US Infantryman in World War II (2)

Mediterranean Theater of Operations 1942–45

Robert S Rush • Illustrated by Elizabeth Sharp & Ian Palmer

First published in Great Britain in 2002 by Osprey Publishing, Elms Court, Chapel Way, Botley, Oxford OX2 9LP, United Kingdom.
Email: info@ospreypublishing.com

ISBN 1 84176 331 4

Editor: Nikolai Bogdanovic
Design: Ken Vail Graphic Design, Cambridge, UK
Index by Alan Rutter
Originated by Magnet Harlequin, Uxbridge, UK
Printed in China through World Print Ltd.

02 03 04 05 06   10 9 8 7 6 5 4 3 2 1

FOR A CATALOG OF ALL BOOKS PUBLISHED BY OSPREY MILITARY AND AVIATION PLEASE CONTACT:

The Marketing Manager, Osprey Direct USA,
c/o MBI Publishing, PO Box 1, 729 Prospect Ave
Osceola, WI 54020, USA.
Email: info@ospreydirectusa.com

The Marketing Manager, Osprey Direct UK, PO Box 140,
Wellingborough, Northants, NN8 2FA, United Kingdom.
Email: info@ospreydirect.co.uk

www.ospreypublishing.com

Artist's note

Readers may care to note that the original paintings from which the colour plates A, B, G and H in this book were prepared are available for private sale. All reproduction copyright whatsoever is retained by the Publishers. All enquiries should be addressed to:

Stanton Graphics,
Stanton Court,
Denton,
Grantham,
Lincs NG32 1JT,
UK

The Publishers regret that they can enter into no correspondence upon this matter.

Author's note

All photos are courtesy of the US Army Signal Corps, National Archives and Records Administration, College Park, Maryland, USA, and the United States Army Center of Military History, Repository of Army Art.

Glossary

1SG	First Sergeant
AUS	Army of the United States
AWOL	Absent Without Leave
BAR	Browning Automatic Rifle
CO	Commanding Officer
EMT	Emergency Medical Tag
ETO	European Theater of Operations
FM	Field Manual
GI	Government Issue
HBT	Herringbone Twill
KIA	Killed In Action
LCV	Landing Craft, Vehicle
LCVP	Landing Craft, Vehicle, Personnel
LST	Landing Ship, Tank
MIA	Missing In Action
MOS	Military Occupational Speciality
MTO	Mediterranean Theater of Operations
NCO	Non-Commissioned Officer
NG	National Guard
OR	Organized Reserve
PSG	Platoon Sergeant
PTO	Pacific Theaters of Operations
RA	Regular Army
ROTC	Reserve Officers, Training Corps
RTC	Replacement Training Center
TO&E	Tables of Organization and Equipment
XO	Executive Officer

FRONT COVER **American soldiers advance through the Tuscan hills in early 1945. (National Archives)**

CONTENTS

US INFANTRYMAN IN WORLD WAR II (2) MEDITERRANEAN THEATER OF OPERATIONS 1942–45

INTRODUCTION

What was astonishing was the speed with which the Americans adapted themselves to modern warfare. In this, they were assisted by their extraordinary sense for the practical and material and by their complete lack of regard for tradition and worthless theories.

Field-Marshal Erwin Rommel, Armeegruppe Afrika

This book is the second in a series that examines the US infantryman in World War II. It provides the reader with a general overview of how American infantrymen in the Mediterranean were organized, equipped, trained and cared for and deals particularly with the problems these soldiers faced while fighting the Germans and Italians in North Africa and Italy.

Rather than fill this book and others in the series with just the dry details of soldiering I have tried to focus on a composite created from actual soldiers and events to examine the reality of daily life and combat in the Mediterranean Theater in 1943–45.

In the course of this book, we follow "John Smith" as he enlists in February 1942, trains at a Replacement Training Center (RTC), and is assigned to the 76th Division. In December 1942 he ships overseas as a replacement, and joins the 133d Regiment in early March 1943 where he fights his first battle in the Fondouk Pass and, more than two years later, his last in the Po Valley of northern Italy.

All military organizations operate under the rubric of regulations and doctrine. Every aspect under which soldiers operate, the uniforms they wear and the weapons they carry are all prescribed by regulation. The different

Young men read the "Defend your country" poster outside their town's recruiting station.

regulations, field manuals, unit reports, and histories written by individual participants all form the basis of our infantryman's narrative. While the focus is on one hypothetical soldier – in fully realistic timescale and experience – the generalities and experiences of the many are also examined and carefully woven into the individual narrative thread. This soldier's experiences include activities similar to those experienced by most replacement infantrymen; his enlistment, testing and selection as an infantryman, training, shipment overseas, promotion and demotion, weapons, injury and illness, as well as the everyday occurrences of eating, resupplying, and fighting across North Africa and Italy.

Between 1940 and 1945 the US Army expanded from eight to 66 infantry divisions. Although the great majority of soldiers filling these units were draftees, many men enlisted during the period immediately after Pearl Harbor. During the hectic days of early 1942 units went overseas with their last maneuvers being those of October 1941, and without any opportunity to correct their deficiencies. National Guard (NG) and Regular Army (RA) divisions traveled overseas first, with most initially going to the Pacific, and the rest earmarked for the campaigns in Europe and North Africa.

The first Army seaborne invasion occurred in November 1942, when three Regular Army infantry divisions (1st, 3d, and 9th, with two sailing from the United States!) and one regiment of the 34th Infantry Division (NG) assaulted North Africa. These organizations were at the optimum personnel strengths, but they lacked advanced training, and much of their necessary modern equipment. Their shortcomings in training and equipment were readily apparent in the opening phases of the Tunisian campaign and casualties were higher than expected. The established RTCs could not keep pace with demand so untrained soldiers in some forming divisions went overseas as replacements.

Warrior 45 *US Infantryman in World War II (1) Pacific Area of Operations 1941–45*, covers in detail the organization and duties of personnel within a rifle company, so it will not be addressed here. This book covers the organization and leadership within the battalion heavy weapons company (D, H, and M companies of an infantry regiment).

	Aug 1, 1942	Jul 15, 1943	Jan 24, 1945
Rifle Battalion (3)	916	871	860
Headquarters (TO 7–16)	4/0	4/0	4/0
Headquarters Co (TO 7–16)	5 off/130 enl-men	5/117	5/117
Company Headquarters	2/29	2/25	2/23
Battalion Headquarters Section	15	13	13
Communications Platoon	1/22	1/22	1/22
Ammunition and Pioneer Platoon	1/23	1/22	1/22
Antitank Platoon	1/41	1/31	1/28
Rifle Co (3) (TO 7–17)	6/192	6/187	6/187
Company Headquarters	2/37	2/33	2/33
Rifle Platoons (3)	1/40	1/40	1/40
Heavy Weapons Platoon	1/35	1/34	1/34
Heavy Weapons Co (TO 7–18)	8/176	8/158	8/152
Company Headquarters	2(3)/35	2(3)/31	2(3)/28
81mm Mortar Platoon	1/59	1/50	1/47
.30 cal. Machine Gun Platoon (2)	1/41	1/35	1/35
Medical Section (from Regimental Medical Detachment)	2/23	3/23	3/23

Infantry Rifle Battalion Table of Organization and Equipment, 1942–45.

THE INFANTRY BATTALION HEAVY WEAPONS COMPANY

Between 1941 and 1945 the heavy weapons company consisted of two .30 caliber machine gun platoons, an 81mm mortar platoon, and a headquarters section split between a command and an administrative group. It was similar to the rifle company, and although equipment and personnel strength changed during the war years, duties and responsibilities of the leaders did not.

The command group consisted of the commanding officer (CO), executive officer (XO), first sergeant (1SG), and reconnaissance/signal sergeant.

The company commander (captain) was responsible for the discipline, administration, supply, training, tactical employment, and control of his company. He decided how best to employ his company in conformity with the battalion commander's scheme of fire support. Although he could listen to advice, he alone was responsible for his organization's success or failure. The reconnaissance officer (lieutenant) was second-in-command. During combat, he reconnoitered for initial and subsequent firing positions, targets, and routes for ammunition resupply. He kept abreast of the company situation and was prepared to assume company command. The 1SG (initially pay grade 2, changed to pay grade 1 in 1944) assisted the company commander in controlling the company. His duties varied from handling administrative and supply matters to maintaining the company command post or commanding a platoon in combat.

The admin group consisted of those headquarters elements not directly involved in the fighting, such as the supply sergeant, transportation sergeant, company clerk, and mess team, of which all except the supply sergeant and transportation sergeant were normally back in the battalion trains area.

.30 Caliber Machine Gun Platoon

The platoon normally consisted of two sections and a command group. The platoon leader (lieutenant) was responsible for the training, discipline, control, and tactical employment of his platoon. In combat, he was responsible for selecting primary, alternate, and supplementary positions; ensuring fire did not endanger troops as well as the delivery of ammunition to the guns. The platoon sergeant (PSG; staff, and later technical sergeant) was second-in-command. He assisted the platoon leader in controlling the platoon and acted as platoon leader when there was no officer present. In combat, the PSG was normally located in the rear of the platoon command post where he could supervise the ammunition bearers. The two corporals assisted in reconnaissance, served as liaison between the platoon and supported company, controlled the fire control equipment, and prepared firing data.

.30 Caliber Machine Gun Section

The section normally consisted of a section sergeant, and two machine gun squads. Each squad had a corporal leader, a machine gunner, an assistant machine gunner, and four ammunition bearers.

The section leader (sergeant, and later staff sergeant) was responsible for their employment, training, and sustenance. In combat he selected and assigned locations for the squads, assigned sectors of fire, and ensured the machine guns remained resupplied. The squad leader (corporal, and later sergeant) selected the exact firing position, observed and adjusted fire, enforced fire discipline, and ensured his ammunition bearers kept his crew resupplied with ammunition.

81mm Mortar Platoon

The duties of the mortar platoon command group were identical to those of the heavy machine gun platoons.

Much like the duties of the section leader in the machine gun platoon the mortar section leader (sergeant and later staff sergeant) was responsible for his squad's employment, training, and sustenance. In combat he selected and assigned locations for the squads, assigned sectors of fire, and ensured the mortars were resupplied. The mortar squad leader (corporal, and later sergeant) selected the exact firing position, observed and adjusted fire. The difference was that usually only one NCO remained with the mortar section to supervise ammunition resupply and the execution of fire commands by the mortar crews. The two other NCOs served as observers for their respective mortars.

Weapons and Weapons Systems

Soldiers in heavy weapons companies carried the same type weapons whether they fought in the Mediterranean (MTO), European (ETO) or Pacific (PTO) theaters of operations. In 1942, the company's primary heavy weapons systems were eight M1917A1 .30 caliber Browning water-cooled heavy machine guns, six M1 81mm mortars, and one M2 .50 caliber Browning air-cooled heavy machine gun. Individual weapons consisted of the .45 caliber automatic pistol, the M1 rifle, and the M1 (and later M2) carbine.

The gunners and assistant gunners carried pistols; the officers, senior NCOs, drivers, and some ammunition bearers the M1 carbine; all others the M1 rifle. Beginning in 1943, each of the three combat platoons received two 2.36-in. bazookas as part of their platoon equipment and these were carried within the platoon headquarters. The heavy weapons company, because of its numerous heavy weapons systems, also contained 19 quarter-ton trucks (jeeps), 14 quarter-ton trailers, and one three-quarter-ton weapons carrier.

Weapons in a Heavy Weapons Company

The M1917A1 .30 caliber heavy machine gun was fully automatic, recoil-operated, and water-cooled, firing a 175-grain bullet to an effective range of 1,100 yards from 250-round belts. The machine gun weight about 93 lbs with tripod and water, and could fire longer, more sustained bursts before overheating than its air-cooled cousins.

The M1 81mm mortar basic design was that of the French Brandt-designed mortar. The mortar weighed 136 lbs and fired rounds weighing between nine and 19 lbs. each, depending whether the round was high explosive (heavy or light), smoke (white phosphorous), or illuminating. The 81mm mortar's range varied depending on the type of shell used, from a minimum of fewer than 200 yards to a maximum of 3,290 yards. Three men could easily carry the mortar for short distances: one carrying the tube, the second the bipod and sight, and the third the base plate.

The M2 .50 caliber heavy machine gun (heavy barrel) was belt-fed, crew-served and air-cooled, and capable of single-shot as well as automatic fire; its functioning was similar to the .30 caliber Browning. The .50 caliber machine gun's primary use was defense against aircraft, with a secondary mission of protecting organic vehicles from ground attack.

THE EFFECTS OF PEARL HARBOR

Most of the men enlisting in the US Army December 1941 through February 1942 did so out of patriotism. The Japanese attack on Pearl Harbor ignited in many a passion for revenge. Although Germany and Italy declared war against the United States on December 11, the main object of American rage was Japan.

Between December 1941 and February 1942 186,360 men enlisted in the US Army. Although the average age of a soldier in 1941 was 26, the newly enlisted soldier was typically younger than the draftee in the next bunk over, with 39.9 percent of those enlisting between the ages of 18 and 21, while only 14.7 percent of the draftees were as young. (Further information on guardsmen can be found in Warrior 45 *US Infantryman in World War II (1) Pacific Area of Operations 1942–45*, and on draftees in Warrior 56 *US Infantryman in World War II (3) European Theater of Operations 1944–45*.)

Anticipating an influx of new soldiers in 1939 and 1940, the War Department had developed standardized training plans for both units and individuals. As the war progressed these were modified and refined, taking on board the most recent information and lessons learned from the overseas combat areas. When training commenced in earnest, a rifleman training at the Infantry Replacement Center at Camp Wheeler, Georgia, received the same hours of instruction on the same subjects as did riflemen training at other Infantry Replacement Centers throughout the country, or for that matter within any of the organizing divisions.

The Mediterranean Theater of Operations

The US Army entered combat in the MTO on November 8, 1942 with ten regiments. Between that date and May 1945, US Army infantry units fought in eight named campaigns in North Africa and Italy.

Although this was the US Army's first major area for offensive operations, it rapidly became a secondary theater for US troops, and strength in the Mediterranean never reached the level of the buildup in Europe or the Pacific.

There were never more than 24 US infantry regiments serving at one time in the MTO. They accumulated 500 months in theater, and 446 combat months between Pearl Harbor on December 7, 1941 and May 2, 1945 – the day the last German forces surrendered in Italy. Strength rose to 18 regiments then dropped to 12 by December 1943, increased to 24 in August 1944, and then fell to 15 in September 1944 with the invasion of southern France.

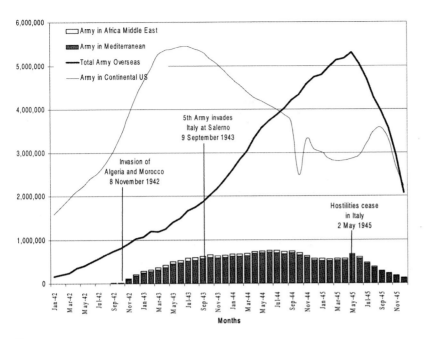

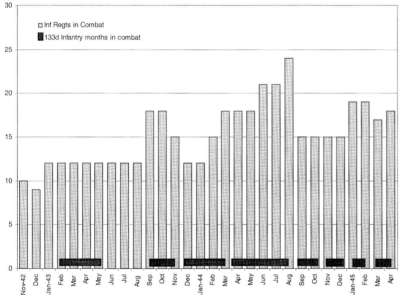

Units remained in the line for extended periods and were subjected to daily losses, if not directly due to combat, then to the terrible weather. As with the PTO, units were short of strength due to a replacement policy which kept soldiers in hospital assigned to their former units and fewer replacements than needed actually reaching units requiring them.

For every soldier felled through combat in the MTO, two others were stricken with disease or nonbattle injuries, and 63 men out of every thousand were hospitalized every day of the campaign. The average daily casualty rate for the US Army was one battle casualty for every four and a half rendered ineffective through disease or nonbattle injury.

The Fifth and Seventh Armies' veteran divisions were deployed to fight in France; with two departing in November/December 1943 and

	Disease	Nonbattle injury	Battle injury or wound	Total Daily admissions per 1,000
Continental US	27.06	4.24	.01	31.31
Africa, Middle East	37.62	6.54	.66	44.82
Mediterranean	33.47	9.59	19.61	62.67

Daily average noneffective rate (per 1,000 strength).

three in August 1944, and were in turn replaced by Organized Reserve (OR) and Army of the United States (AUS) divisions arriving from America. Only the 34th Infantry Division (NG) remained in the MTO from beginning to end.

The Organized Reserve and Army of the United States

Unlike the National Guard, the OR was a Federal organization. During the interwar years, the OR divisions were skeletons consisting primarily of WW I era officers with the junior grades filled by Reserve Officers' Training Corps (ROTC) graduates. There was little opportunity to train with troops and, like NG officers, the Reserve officers kept abreast of their speciality by taking correspondence courses that qualified them for promotion.

All of the 39 infantry divisions organized in the US after Pearl Harbor in 1942 and 1943 were components of the OR or AUS. They were built around the cadre concept; an older more established division provided officers and soldiers who became the organization and training element for the new division. The new division's junior officers came from officer candidate and service schools while the great majority of its enlisted men came directly from reception centers. Germany used this same process in forming new divisions in late 1940 and early 1941.

The Army Ground Forces estimated that divisions required 10–12 months' training to be fully prepared for combat. Responsibility for training rested with commanders, who continually emphasized those tasks necessary for basic mission accomplishment, stressing drills and techniques for the small units. They wanted soldiers to be able to walk before they ran. Training progressed through four phases: basic and individual training – 17 weeks devoted to individual up through battalion level training; 13 weeks of unit training primarily at regimental level; 14

Campaigns in the Mediterranean Theater of Operations.

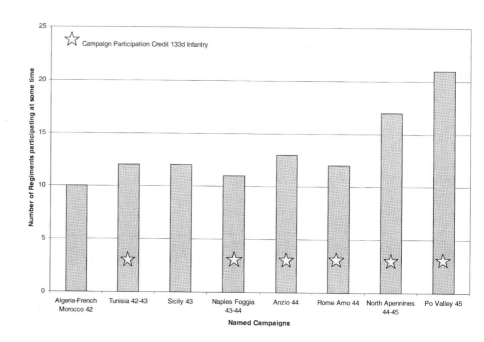

Soldiers in dungarees fire M1903 Springfields on an unimproved range in 1940/41. A coach kneels on the firer's right, observing the strike of the round as well as the firer's body position. Note not only the sparseness of the range, but also its size, large enough for a battalion to fire in one order.

weeks of combined arms training, which included at least one division against division maneuver. Another eight weeks were devoted to review.

Every division organized after 1941 had at least one year of training and most more, although many divisions suffered severe personnel upheaval with soldiers leaving as replacements as soon as they were basically trained. All except one division saw combat in 1944 and 1945 with five in the MTO, six in the PTO, and 27 in the ETO.

The 76th Infantry Division, one of the divisions of the OR (of which our soldier, John Smith, was a part for about five months), was activated in June 1942 from a small cadre of 185 Regular and Reserve officers and 1,190 enlisted men, most of whom were specialists in the different technical services. There were not enough NCOs to fill all the positions and consequently many newly trained graduates of the RTCs found themselves rapidly promoted to NCO positions with no military background outside their 13 weeks of training. Due to the massive upheaval both in forming new units and filling units preparing to go overseas, the 76th Division was designated a Replacement Pool Division in October 1942. Unit training stopped and concentration was placed instead on housing soldiers until it was their turn to ship overseas as replacements. Some recruits who arrived from reception centers in June and July 1942 to fill the forming division received very little infantry training before shipping overseas to North Africa, and this ultimately created a great uproar overseas.

Unit training began again in March 1943 when the 76th Division refilled and restarted its basic training cycle. Twenty-two months later, in January 1945, the division shipped overseas to France and entered combat immediately.

By September 1942 all infantry organizations within the rifle regiment were identical by Tables of Organization and Equipment (TO&E). Most had to make do with antiquated equipment in 1942 until production caught up and units received their full authorization of new equipment. Overseas divisions might have modified clothing issues for soldiers fighting in the different climates, but weapons and manpower were identical to those in the United States.

RIGHT **The route of the 133d Infantry Regiment in the Mediterranean Theater of Operations.**

Our composite soldier

Our soldier, John Smith, was born in northern Georgia and enlisted at age 19 in January 1942. John's father was a hard-scrabble dirt farmer, like many in the triangular area where the states of Georgia, Alabama, and Tennessee touched. His mother probably died birthing the youngest of the children, now a six-year-old girl. John had an eighth grade education, a little higher than normal for a boy growing up on a farm during the 1930s. Like many during the Great Depression, he had left school to help his father and brothers work the farm. In 1940 and 1941 John's brothers left to find work in defense plants. With his brothers gone it was difficult for him and his father to work the plot of land with the few farm implements they had. There was seldom enough to eat and their diet was poor. After Pearl Harbor, John decided to join the Army but since he was only 19 he had to get his father's permission.

John trained at an RTC and was initially assigned to the newly formed 76th Infantry Division (OR). He was later assigned overseas to North Africa as a replacement to the 1st Battalion 133d Infantry Regiment, 34th Infantry Division ("Red Bull") after one of the battalion's companies suffered heavy losses recapturing Kef-al-Ahmar Pass.

The 133d Infantry Regiment

The 133d Infantry Regiment (Iowa Army National Guard) was federalized along with its parent 34th Infantry Division on February 10, 1941. Its first batallion arrived in Northern Ireland on January 26, 1942, less than a month and a half after Pearl Harbor. The 34th Infantry Division was the only original US division landing in North Africa to spend its entire war in the MTO, with one of its regiments beginning active combat on November 8, 1942 when it landed west of Algiers. The remainder of the division landed in North Africa on January 2, 1943. Major engagements at Fondouk and Hill 609 followed, and after a period of retraining, they landed at Salerno, Italy, on September 21, 1943. The 133d Infantry Regiment spent the next 19 months fighting up the "boot" of Italy, which included crossing the Volturno River three times, San Angelo D'Alife, Cassino, Anzio, Rome, Cecina, the Arno River, the Gothic Line, and the final battles in the Po Valley in spring 1945.

The 133d Infantry Regiment remained in Europe throughout the summer of 1945 and returned to the United States with its parent division in October that year where it inactivated on November 3, 1945, after serving overseas for 45 months.

CHRONOLOGY

During the 1930s and 1940s, most people received their information about America's approach to war through reading their town or city newspaper, and by listening to the radio. When war came and soldiers shipped overseas to the Mediterranean, they read the Mediterranean edition of the *Stars and Stripes* newspaper and listened to the BBC.

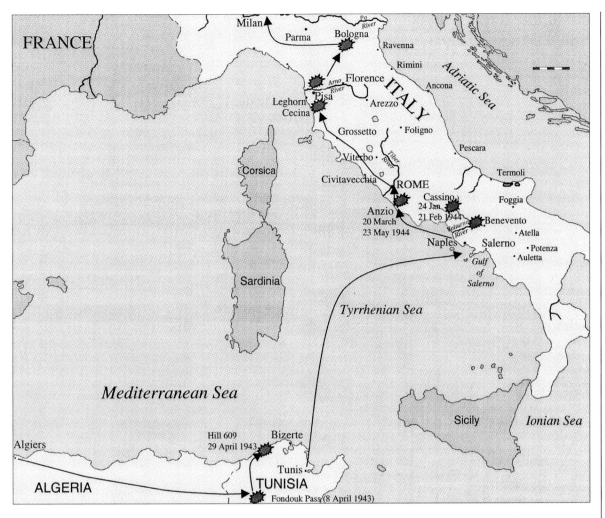

Jan 30, 1933	Adolf Hitler appointed German Chancellor	**Mar 24, 1941**	Axis (Rommel) takes El Agheila
1935–36	Italy conquers Ethiopia; 1936–39 Spanish Civil War	**Apr 9, 1941**	Axis captures Bardia
		Apr 10, 1941	Axis siege of Tobruk begins
Mar 12, 1938	German Anschluss of Austria	**Apr 22, 1941**	British begin withdrawal from Greece
May 22, 1939	Germany and Italy sign "Pact of Steel"	**Apr 23, 1941**	Greek Army surrenders to Germans
		Apr 27, 1941	Axis occupies Halfaya Pass
Aug 23, 1939	Soviet–German Nonaggression Pact signed	**May 2, 1941**	British complete evacuation from Greece
Sep 1, 1939	Germany invades Poland – The war in Europe begins	**May 20, 1941**	Germans invade Crete
		Jun 1, 1941	British complete evacuation of Crete
Nov 3, 1939	US Congress passes "cash and carry" amendment to Neutrality Laws	**Jun 15, 1941**	British launch Operation Battleaxe offensive in Western Desert
Aug 15, 1940	Eagle Day – Battle of Britain	**Jul 5, 1941**	US forces begin occupying Iceland
Sep 13, 1940	Italian Army advances into Egypt	**Aug 9–12, 1941**	Roosevelt and Churchill meet in Atlantic Conference. Atlantic Charter proclaimed
Sep 16, 1940	Selective Service Act signed		
Nov 5, 1940	Roosevelt elected to third term as US President		
		Oct 31, 1941	The destroyer USS *Reuben James* sunk by U-boat
Dec 9, 1940	British attack Italians in Western Desert, Egypt	**Nov 18, 1941**	British open Crusader desert offensive
Jan 22, 1941	British capture Tobruk, Libya	**Nov 30, 1941**	British 8th Army links up with Tobruk garrison
Feb 5, 1941	British victorious at Beda Fomm		
Feb 12, 1941	Rommel arrives in Tripoli, Libya	**Dec 7, 1941**	Japanese attack Pearl Harbor
Mar 11, 1941	US Lend-Lease Act signed	**Dec 8, 1941**	United States declares war on Japan

Dec 10, 1941	Siege of Tobruk is lifted	
Dec 11, 1941	Germany and Italy declare war on United States, which takes reciprocal action	
Dec 24, 1941	British re-enter Benghazi	
Dec 24 to Jan 14, 1941	Arcadia Conference in Washington	
Jan 1, 1942	Declaration of the United Nations signed	
Jan 17, 1942	Halfaya garrison surrenders to British	
Jan 22, 1942	In new Axis offensive, Rommel retakes Agedabia	
Jan 26, 1942	1st Battalion 133d Infantry, elements of the first division (34th) sent to the European Theater arrive in Northern Ireland.	
May 27, 1942	Rommel attacks Gazala Line in large-scale Axis offensive	
Jun 17, 1942	British withdrawal in Libya leaves Tobruk isolated	
Jun 21, 1942	Tobruk falls to Rommel's forces	
Jun 28, 1942	Axis takes Mersa Matrüh in Egypt	
Jul 1–17, 1942	First battle of El Alamein	
Aug 22, 1942	Brazil declares war on Germany and Italy	
Aug 31 to Sep 7, 1942	Battle of Alam Halfa	
Sep 12, 1942	Eisenhower assumes post as C-in-C Allied Expeditionary Force (for Northwest Africa)	
Oct 23 to Nov 4, 1942	Second battle of El Alamein	
Nov 3, 1942	Axis begins retreat at El Alamein	
Nov 8, 1942	Allies land in Northwest Africa (Operation Torch)	
Nov 11, 1942	Germans occupy southern France	
Nov 11, 1942	British 8th Army takes Bardia	
Nov 11, 1942	French cease resistance in Northwest Africa	
Nov 13, 1942	British take Tobruk	
Dec 13, 1942	Axis begins retreat from Al Agheila	
Jan 14–23, 1943	Allied Casablanca Conference begins	
Jan 15, 1943	British 8th Army opens drive on Tripoli	
Feb 19, 1943	Axis attacks at Kasserine Pass	
Mar 1, 1943	Von Arnim replaces Rommel as Axis C-in-C in Africa	
Mar 26, 1943	British 8th Army breaks through Mareth Line	
Mar 27–31, 1943	34th Infantry Division begins attack on Fondouk Pass but fails in effort	
Apr 8, 1943	1st Battalion 133d Infantry begins attack at Fondouk Pass	
Apr 30, 1943	Elements of 34th Infantry Division seize Hill 609	
May 7, 1943	Allied 18th Army Group captures Tunis and Bizerte	
May 7, 1943	Axis forces in northeast Tunisia surrender unconditionally	
May 12–25, 1943	Trident Conference (Anglo-American) begins in Washington. All Axis resistance in North Africa ends	
Jul 10, 1943	Allies invade Sicily	
Jul 22, 1943	Palermo falls to US 7th Army	
Jul 25, 1943	Mussolini resigns; Badoglio becomes	

	Italian Prime Minister
Aug 14–24, 1943	First Quebec Conference
Sep 3, 1943	British 8th Army lands on Calabrian coast of Italy
Sep 8, 1943	Eisenhower announces Italian surrender
Sep 9, 1943	US 5th Army lands at Salerno, Italy
Sep 10, 1943	German forces occupy Rome
Sep 22, 1943	133d Infantry lands at Salerno
Oct 12, 1943	US 5th Army attacks across Volturno River; 133d Infantry's first crossing of Volturno River
Oct 13, 1943	Italy declares war on Germany
Oct 18, 1943	133d Infantry's second crossing of Volturno River
Nov 4, 1943	133d Infantry's third crossing of Volturno River
Nov 5, 1943	Allies begin assaults on Winter Line in Italy
Nov 22–26, 1943	Allied Cairo Conference
Nov 28–30, 1943	Allied 'Big Three' attend Teheran Conference
Dec 3–7, 43	Allied meetings resume at Cairo
Jan 15, 1944	Winter Line Campaign ends
Jan 22, 1944	US 5th Army lands at Anzio
Jan 24 to Feb 21, 1944	34th Infantry Division begins its battle for Cassino
Feb 15, 1944	Allies bomb abbey of Monte Cassino
Mar 25, 1944	133d Infantry lands at Anzio
May 11, 1944	Allies open drive on Rome with attack on Gustav Line
May 23, 1944	US 5th Army breaks out at Anzio beachhead
Jun 3, 1944	Lanuvio falls to 133d Infantry
Jun 4, 1944	US 5th Army enters Rome
Jun 6, 1944	Allies invade Normandy, France (Operation Overlord)
Aug 3, 1944	British 8th Army takes Florence
Aug 9, 1944	Eisenhower establishes HQ in France
Sep 10, 1944	5th Army begins attack on Gothic Line
Sep 21, 1944	British 8th Army takes Rimini
Oct 16, 1944	133d Infantry attacks Mount Belmonte (to Oct 23, 1943)
Nov 7, 1944	Roosevelt elected to fourth term as US President
Feb 4–11, 1945	Yalta Conference
Apr 12, 1945	Roosevelt dies; Truman succeeds as US President
Apr 14, 1945	Allies begin major attack on Gothic Line (Italy)
Apr 21, 1945	133d Infantry takes Bologna
Apr 25, 1945	United Nations conference opens in San Francisco
Apr 28, 1945	Mussolini is executed by partisans
May 2,1945	German forces surrender in Italy
May 7, 1945	All German forces surrender unconditionally (0241 hrs at Reims)
May 8, 1945	Proclaimed VE Day
Oct 1945	133d Infantry Regiment returns to the United States
Nov 3, 1945	133d Infantry Regiment inactivated

JOHN'S ENLISTMENT, RECEPTION AND INITIAL TRAINING

John's family didn't read much besides the Bible, and they received most news from a neighbor who had a radio. They heard of the attack on Pearl Harbor and the United States' entry into the war in this way. The more John heard, the more he wanted to enlist. He was too young to register for the draft, and was afraid the war would be over before he was drafted. Moreover, he wanted to earn money for his family to tide them over until things improved. With the draft and many people leaving to work in defense factories, there were few hands to help in the fields come planting season, which meant that fewer acres would be planted and the next year would be a hungry one for his family.

The small town John lived near didn't have a recruiting station, or any other military presence for that matter, so in January 1942 he walked and hitchhiked to the nearest town with a recruiting station to enlist. There he found that since he was under 21, his father had to sign a waiver for him to enlist and there was no enlistment bonus. The recruiter gave him a round trip bus ticket to travel home and back.

In February, John returned to the station with his birth certificate and his father's very carefully block-printed letter. He then took a preliminary physical, which he almost failed because he weighed only 120lbs, low for a 5 ft 10 in. frame, and *did* fail because his teeth were in poor shape – enough so that he was deferred from enlisting until the worst teeth were fixed. After a note from the recruiter to a local dentist, three teeth were pulled and John was ready to proceed.

Having met the basic physical qualifications to be a soldier, he boarded a bus along with other enlistees and inductees from the area for the trip to Fort McPherson, Georgia.

The men were put into formation as soon as they got off the bus, and had to quickly learn the position of the soldier: head erect, chin in, eyes looking straight to the front; body erect, chest lifted and arched, shoulders squared, arms hanging with palms in and thumbs along the seams of the trousers; heels together, and feet turned out at 45 degrees. From the bus they gaggle-marched to the mess hall for their first US Army meal of fried chicken, mashed potatoes, beans, coleslaw, milk, coffee, and apple pie. The sign in the mess hall stated: "TAKE ALL YOU WANT, EAT ALL YOU TAKE." At the time soldiers received about 4,500 calories a day, or about 1,000 to 2,500 calories more than most well-fed civilians, and it was much more than John had enjoyed as a civilian.

After "chow," the men filed into brand-new barracks of unfinished wood for the night, where the beds were single bunked, head to foot to prevent the spread of meningitis.

They received their first lesson in making a bed US Army style. The corporal demonstrated by first tucking in the head sheet, then making hospital (45 degree) corners by pulling up the edge of the sheet about 15 in. from the end of the bed and lifting it up so it made a diagonal fold, laying the fold onto the mattress and tucking the hanging part of the sheet under the mattress. He then dropped the fold, pulling it smooth and tucking it under the mattress, following at the foot with the same procedure for the top sheet and blanket, except beginning at the foot.

The next day, John underwent another, more thorough physical. Some who had passed the physical in their hometown were disqualified and sent home by the Army doctors. An officer administered a literacy test that tested to fourth grade level those who had not completed high school. Some of the boys who arrived with John could not read, so they were given a verbal test to determine whether they could follow instructions. Those who failed all the tests were interviewed, and if found not to be malingering, they were sent home.

After passing the medical and literacy tests, those remaining received their serial numbers which identified them from other soldiers of the same name, and which would stay with them the remainder of their service. There were two lines, both in alphabetical order but with brothers separated, one for draftees and one for enlistees. As an enlistee, John's number began with a 14, the first number signifying he had enlisted, the second designating the corps area in which he had enlisted. The other six numbers were corps numbers generally indicating when a soldier enlisted; the lower the number the earlier in the war a soldier had signed up.

How to read World War II era Regular Army serial numbers. Arizona (AZ) appears twice because it was split between two service areas.

RA prior to Sept 1940 (7 digits)	6, 7		2d through 7th digit allocated by corps area. Normally the lower the number, the earlier the entry on active duty.
RA after Sept 1940	1		2d through 8th digit allocated by Service Command. The lower the number, the earlier the entry on active duty.
		1	1st Corps Area (ME, NH, VT, MA, RI, CT)
		2	2d Corps Area (NJ, DE, NY)
		3	3d Corps Area (PA, MD, VA, DC)
		4	4th Corps Area (NC, SC, GA, FL, AL, TN, MS, LA)
		5	5th Corps Area (OH, WV, IN, KY)
		6	6th Corps Area (IL, MI, WI)
		7	7th Corps Area (MO, KS, AR, IA, NB, MN, ND, SD, WY)
		8	8th Corps Area (TX, OK, CO, NM, AZ)
		9	9th Corps Area (WA, OR, ID, MT, UT, NV, CA, AZ)

John then – with several hundred other boys and men, draftees, and enlistees alike – raised his right hand to swear the Oath of Enlistment. John noticed that most of the men were in their twenties. He raised his right hand and swore the following oath:

"I _____ do solemnly swear (or affirm) that I will bear true faith and allegiance to the United States of America; that I will serve them honestly and faithfully against all their enemies whomsoever; and that I will obey the President of the United States and the orders of the officers appointed over me according to the rules and Articles of War."

The next few days passed rapidly, transforming civilians into recruits, with continuous testing to determine what the men were best suited for; they were read the Articles of War, issued with uniforms, and taught the rudiments of drill; all before they were shipped to their training location.

Soldiers display their newly-issued clothing, as the NCO calls off each item.

The classification tests determined mechanical aptitude and general IQ – after which the new soldiers were interviewed for job qualifications. John scored an 80 of a possible 160 on his test, which placed him mid-range in Category IV and about average for someone with eighth grade schooling; those with better education and reading ability normally scored higher, although this was not always the case. The different classes were Class I (over 130) very superior; Class II (110 and over) superior; Class III (109 to 90) average; Class IV (89 to 70) inferior; and Class V (69 and below) very inferior.

As an enlistee in January 1942, John could volunteer for any skill the Army contained if he were qualified. However, after taking the tests and being interviewed by a classification specialist, he opted for the Infantry over the other branches he was offered – Quartermaster and Engineers – as the Infantry Branch seemed more exciting than the other two.

Next came clothing issue and John and his fellow enlistees formed a line going into a long building. It was like an extended assembly line. The soldiers slowly walked down a long counter where the clerks, after a quick glance as to build, piled the new soldiers' arms with uniforms of all sorts: two-piece herringbone twill (HBT) work clothes; khakis, raincoat, overcoat, caps, underclothes, socks, dress shoes, service shoes, and canvas leggings. John now had more clothing than he had ever owned at one time in his life. He was especially impressed with his service shoes: a clerk had measured them to fit his feet while he wore army socks and held a bucket of sand in each hand. A soldier in 1942 walked much more than he rode, and a soldier falling by the wayside due to a foot injury was as serious a loss to his unit as a soldier who was wounded.

John and his comrades then stood in line for a series of inoculations; smallpox, typhoid fever, and tetanus. They were all read the Articles of War which, the officer explained, were no more than common-sense rules necessary for good order and discipline. John especially remembered the articles concerning company punishment where a commander could withhold privileges and administer extra duty for one week for offenses not warranting a court-martial; absent without leave, for being away from his assigned place of duty without permission; desertion, for leaving one's post without intention of returning; neglecting equipment, for losing, selling, or neglecting to take care of his equipment; misconduct, for being drunk and disorderly, writing bad checks, lending money for interest, and a host of other minor offenses. John realized the seriousness of the Articles when he learned that the

strongest penalties were for desertion and divulging military secrets, both of which were death.

The next morning everyone fell out for their first taste of calisthenics, and then watched movies on venereal disease. That afternoon, John found his name on the company bulletin board for shipment to the Infantry Replacement Training Center at Camp Wheeler, Georgia. Before they departed on the train there was yet another physical inspection, this time to catch any cases of gonorrhea that might have escaped detection so far.

Spartan World War II era barracks. The beds are arranged head-to-toe, and beneath them are soldiers' shoes: foot lockers are placed along the center isle. Field gear and clothing were placed on shelves and pegs mounted on the walls.

Camp Wheeler

On arrival at Camp Wheeler, John and his comrades were quarantined for 72 hours to ensure there was no infectious meningitis in the group. John and his comrades received their issue of infantry equipment that included an M1903 Springfield rifle, pack, cartridge belt, canteen, tent-half, mess kit, and gas mask. The individual equipment was stored on pegs near his bunk and his rifle was in one of the circular gun racks placed down the center aisle of the barracks.

Everyone received a short haircut during the first week of training. Each day except Sunday began with First Call at 0630hrs and Reveille at 0645hrs. A daily schedule was busy from the start. Make up bunk, wash, dress, fall out to the barracks, across the road to the mess hall at 0700hrs, sit at the table until whistle is blown, turn over plate, fill plate, start eating. Then calisthenics in undershirts, back to the barracks to sweep and mop. Out into the street at 0845hrs for manual of arms, close-order drill, or weapons training. Back to the company area for lunch; out into the field for afternoon training. Back to the barracks at 1745hrs, dress in khaki uniform for retreat. Supper at 1845 hrs after retreat, and evenings free until 2400hrs, but lights out and Taps played at 2200hrs. Saturdays were different; everyone prepared for and stood a parade and then inspection, and if everything was shipshape, they were allowed on pass beginning at noon.

John was surprised at the different kinds of people in his training company. His company was principally from the East Coast and South, although some were from as far away as Maine, and like him, many were farmers. Some were mill workers, others had been clerks or salesmen, and there were a few professional musicians and educated white-collar professionals. Education ranged from almost none to post-graduate level. The more technical branches had little need for the men steeped in the humanities or salesmen, and many ended up in the different combat arms branches. It appeared that only those with technical skills or craftsmen were not represented – they were more likely to be in the Ordnance Corps, the Engineers, or one of the other technical branches. Many of those from small southern farms, including John, had never driven a car and, unlike the men from the cities and towns, were mechanically illiterate. All of the recruits were single.

As one of the younger men, John listened to the talk of those who were older. "If a bullet has my name on it, it'll get me" was a popular philosophy. Most, including John, did not want to lie around camps for two or three years; they wanted to see immediate action, and if they were destined to die they did not want to languish in boredom until it happened. It seemed as if everything was happening in the Pacific. Thirteen weeks seemed long enough to prepare for combat.

John and the other recruits saw their officers only during training. In 1942, most officers at the training centers were either too old for front-line duty or brand-new second lieutenants. The recruits all felt a certain air about the "90-day wonders" who were present at much of their training. Many preferred the older, gray, mustachioed lieutenants who appeared to have an inordinate amount of patience and who didn't seem to rely so much on threats to get things done. But it was the noncommissioned officers, living in the NCO rooms at the end of their barracks, that kept them in line and focused on learning to be a soldier and who, if crossed, could make life miserable for a young soldier. Anyone thought to be "goldbricking" or trying to pull the wool over one of the NCOs' eyes was in for a very long day, although most probably these same NCOs attempted the same tricks when they were young privates. It was all a matter of learning the ropes.

Later, when the new recruits were allowed on pass into nearby Macon, they had to show the pack of prophylactics they were carrying before signing out. The Army considered those who did not return from pass AWOL, and after payday, there were usually several men from each company absent. The penalty at Camp Wheeler was a summary court-martial, which usually adjudged three days guardhouse for every day AWOL.

In the beginning, it seemed the recruits watched training films almost every day. The first film featured graphic pictures of advanced cases of venereal disease and the Army's preventative instructions. Others were on customs, courtesies, and Army regulations; the reason the United States was fighting; plus a myriad of other classroom-type instructions. Frequently, practical application followed what they had learned on the screen.

By the second week of basic training, the men began learning about their areas of specialty; specialties that were assigned to the men based on the interviews. John found himself training to be a heavy machine gunner, Military Occupational Specialty (MOS) 605. His training company contained soldiers training to be heavy machine gunners, and mortar men. Other companies trained soldiers to be infantrymen in rifle companies. Most of the training was similar, only diverging with weapons training. John's company only familiarized with the M1, M1903 rifles, and the Browning Automatic Rifle (BAR), while qualifying on the machine gun or mortar, and familiarizing with the other weapons. Those in the training rifle companies, dependent upon MOS, qualified with the weapon of their duty description, and more of them got to throw the hand grenade. During this period of the war, there was not enough training ammunition to qualify every man on every weapon. Later, in 1943, recruits had more than enough ammunition to fire.

John's company practiced throwing blue-painted practice grenades into windows and trenches on a grenade course during the second week. John and his comrades all wanted to throw a live grenade but the sergeant selected only one to do so. Everyone got down behind a berm while the recruit went alone to the grenade pit. They watched him take the grenade in his right hand, pull the pin with his left, and heave the grenade "in a graceful arching motion." A wait of a few seconds, then a cascade of dirt, and the boom of the explosion.

Next came pistol familiarization. The recruits were handed an M1917 .45 caliber Smith & Wesson revolver, shown how to aim, and with the admonition not to flinch because "it was nothing but a gun" they

Officer and Enlisted Military Occupational Specialties within an Infantry Regiment.

Officer MOS	Description	Location	Officer MOS	Description	Location
200	Communications Officer	HQs	605	Heavy MG gunner	Hv Wpns
600	Motor Transport Officer	Svc Co	607	Mortar gunner	Rifle and Hv Wpns
1189	Artillery Observer, Forward	CN Co	608	Gun pointer	Cannon Co
1192	Cannon Commander, Infantry	CN Co	609	Antitank gunner	Bn HQs and AT
1424	Antitank Unit Commander	AT Co	631	Intelligence NCO	HQs
1542	Infantry Unit Commander	Rifle, Bn, and Rgt	651	Platoon Sergeant	All
1930	Combat Liaison Officer	HQs	652	Section Leader	All
2162	S3 Ops and Tng Officer	HQs	653	Squad Leader	All
2260	S1 Personnel Staff Officer	HQs	657	Litter Bearer	Med Det
2622	Unit Officer Training Center	HQs	666	First Aid man	Med Det
2900	HQ Co Commander	RHHC	667	Message Center Clerk	HQs
2901	HQ Commandant	RHQ	673	Medical NCO	Med Det
2910	Service Co Commander	Svc Co	674	Message Center Chief	HQs
4010	S4 Sup and Evac Officer	Svc Co	675	Messenger	All
5310	Chaplain	RHQ	676	Message Dispatcher	HQs
9301	S2 Intelligence Staff Officer	HQs	729	Pioneer	HQs
9312	Reconnaissance Officer	HQs	734	Halftrack driver	HQs and AT
60	Cook	All	744	Reconnaissance NCO	HQs and AT
501	Admin and tech clerk	HQs	745	Rifleman	Rifle Co
55	Clerk General	HQs	746	Automatic Rifleman	Rifle Co
56	Mail Clerk	All	760	Scout	HQs
345	Truck Driver, Light	All	811	Antitank NCO	Bn HQs and AT
502	Admin NCO	HQs	812	Heavy weapons NCO	Hv Wpns Cos
504	Ammo handler	HQs and Sep Co	814	Operations NCO	HQs
505	Ammunition NCO	HQs and Sep Co	815	Ordnance NCO	HQs
511	Armorer	All	816	Personnel NCO	HQs
521	Basic	All	821	Supply NCO	All
531	Cannoneer	Cannon Co	824	Mess Sergeant	All
585	First Sergeant	All	835	Supply Clerk	All
604	Light MG gunner	Rifle Co			

fired their 20 rounds at targets positioned 15 and 25 yds away. John scored a 110 of a possible 200 points, just a bit above average for his platoon.

Soon thereafter, John's company fell out with gas masks and marched down the dusty road to the gas chamber. There they lined up, put on and cleared their masks, buttoned the top button on their HBTs, and walked into the chamber. Once inside, John noticed that his skin burned a bit, but he was able to breathe without difficulty. When ordered to remove his mask, his eyes, nose, and throat began burning; he, along with the others, rushed out the door and into the fresh air. After everyone had experienced the sulfur trioxide (FS), the men filed in again to practice donning their masks in a chemical environment. The instructor released the chloracetophenone (CN) which John noticed had an odor of apple blossoms and made his eyes burn, immediately producing tears; he and his comrades held their breath until the instructor announced "Mask!" Everyone rapidly donned and cleared their masks, and then stood steady in the gas-filled room. It was quickly apparent which soldiers had not properly put on and cleared their masks when they ran for the door. The remainder filed out.

Lungs still burning a bit, they spent the remainder of the day sniffing cloths containing the scents of the different gases. Any hesitation or uncertainty in a gas environment meant death or debilitating injury. Lewisite (M1) smelled of geraniums, and blistered skin and lungs; chlorpicrin (PS) had a strong odor of licorice or fly paper and was a skin, eye, and respiratory irritant; mustard gas (H) smelled like garlic, attacked the eyes and lungs, and caused blisters on the skin; phosgene (CG) smelled of new-mown hay, caused severe nausea, vomiting, chest

Soldiers check the fitting and seal of their M1A1 service gas mask prior to entering the gas chamber.

pain, shortness of breath, and headaches. At the end of the long day, the instructors made John and his comrades don their masks and march the six miles back to barracks in them.

They ran the 100-yd obstacle course during the third week. The men competed against one another in a contest to finish first. The course involved hurdling two fences, running through a maze, scaling an eight-foot high wall, crawling under a trestle, leaping across a ditch, running across elevated wood beams, and then sprinting to the finish line. Lanky as he was – but weighing about 15 lbs more than he had a little more than a month previous – John was able to finish in the top ten of his platoon.

Later, in the ninth week, John and his company negotiated another much more grueling course. This time it was using a rope to climb up and over a 12ft wall and dropping to the other side. Next, up a slanting ladder; across a log; jumping through a framework of logs; running, grabbing a rope, and swinging over a water-filled ditch; crossing another ditch using hand-over-hand along parallel bars about 10 ft above the water. Then through a small tunnel; over a series of log obstacles, and through wire entanglements; this all run at full speed with officers encouraging them at each obstacle. After a quick breather the recruits ran it a second time.

With gas rationing in effect, the men marched everywhere. While training on the machine gun range, they marched three miles out after breakfast, hand-carrying the machine guns; three miles back for lunch, three miles out again after lunch; and when the day was done three miles back again carrying the machine guns. John was in good shape, so the marches really did not affect him, although he got his share of blisters while breaking his shoes in.

During the third week, the men began to march with fully loaded haversacks. One day they began marching at 0830hrs with full equipment and had covered 10 miles by 1030hrs. They marched another five miles after lunch, and then double-timed for 24 minutes. When they returned from this speed march, the soldiers stretched out on their bunks with bare feet for the medics to check their blisters.

John's real problem was refolding his tent-half and blanket into an envelope roll within the time specified. He was not alone, however. For the life of him, he could not make head or tail of the instructions in the *Soldier's Handbook*, and neither could some of the educated types. It was down to practice with the first few tries looking like overstuffed sausage rolls.

Although John's primary weapon later would be a heavy machine gun and pistol, during training he carried an M1903 Springfield rifle, as all infantrymen were riflemen first. He and his comrades trained in the intricacies of the Springfield rifle in their section of the parade field, learning the names and descriptions of each part, disassembly, assembly, then sighting exercises and dry-fire practice from the prone position. Like many of the other men from the farm, John had grown up around rifles and considered himself a crack shot. He found the Army way of firing rifles to be quite different and difficult, especially the way he had to twist his body and wrap the weapon's sling around his arm to achieve the required firing position.

John's company fired the M1903 Springfield, the M1 rifle and the M1918A1 BAR during the fourth week of training. His first rounds with the M1903 were at every quadrant of the target as he tried to adjust his body to his rifle. An officer observed his problem and let him fire without the sling,

Two M1917A1 heavy machine gun platoons practice timed crew drill.

and John hit the target every time. However, for all the time on the rifle range, John fired fewer than 50 rounds in total. Much of the remaining time he spent in the rifle pits, pulling and marking targets while others fired. He heard that the recruits training as riflemen fired many more rounds from the M1 and BAR, qualifying with each. John's firing was just for familiarization. He would have to qualify on the machine gun.

John found to his relief that his machine gun training was more by practice than by lecture. They watched a training film on assembly and disassembly of the M1917A1 Browning heavy machine gun, then they took one apart, naming each piece, and reassembled it. This progressed to the point where the recruits could take the M1917A1 apart and put it back together blindfolded. They also learned to set the weapon's headspace and timing by feel, while their instructors told them they might have to change barrels during the night in the heat of combat.

Next came crew drill, or putting the machine gun into operation. After a five-minute demonstration by the cadre, the corporal instructor broke the recruits into groups of three for crew drill, numbering the men in the groups from one to three. The corporal gave the commands, the number one man snapped the tripod in place, the number two brought up the gun and placed it into position on the tripod, and the number three hurried forward with the water container and ammunition box. Then they rotated positions until every man had practiced each position.

Unfortunately for some, it was not just hands-on learning. Besides the practical work, they had to learn to use the traversing and elevating (T&E) mechanism in precision firing, studying the firing tables when planning the use of the machine gun in both indirect role and when firing over the heads of friendly troops.

John quickly learned what a mil represented – one mil at 1,000 yards equaled one yard of deviation, and that there were 6,400 mils in 360 degrees. The M18A1 tripod had a 6,400-mil traversing dial, scribed in 20-mil increments, that the machine gun cradle rested on. The traversing and elevating mechanism was located at the rear of the cradle. Using the mechanism, John found he could traverse left and right in 50-mil increments and fine tune direction one mil at a time; thus he could elevate the weapon up to 65 degrees, or 1,156 mils, in 50 and one mil increments.

Like many of his comrades, John had to visualize the movement of the barrel when zeroing and setting preplanned targets on the T&E

mechanism, so that he did not lay the gun in the direction opposite the direction he wanted the rounds to strike. Another of John's concerns was understanding the firing tables for the ammunition the machine gun fired, the calculations within necessary for computing the gunner's rule for firing over the heads of friendly troops.

The machine gun range, to which they normally marched four times a day was three miles from camp: out and back for lunch, and out and back for supper. Sometimes the mess sergeant brought their chow out, and they ate out of mess kits, but that was not often. They spent hours and days on machine guns, dry shooting and learning to coordinate the multiple actions needed to handle the guns while firing. John found the instructors were competent, and very patient with those to whom the mechanical training did not come easily. When they returned to barracks after dinner, many times the machine guns were set up so the men could practice. The large influx of draftees had not yet arrived at the training centers and the onus was on properly training soldiers.

While they practiced manipulating the T&E, they also practiced the machine gun fire commands. The corporal would call out the six elements of the initial fire command: the alert (fire mission), direction (front, front right, etc.), description (dismounted troops), range (700), method of fire (traverse, search, traverse and search; engagement: slow-, rapid-, or quick-fire), and the command to open fire (fire, or, at my command) with the gun crews repeating each element as it was given.

Then they fired for record on the 1,000-in. range with the silhouettes scaled so that they represented men at 441 yds. John had to traverse and search the different targets designated on the paster; some series of targets ran horizontally across the target, others diagonally, and still others vertically. He was just able to make out the strike of the rounds on the target and adjusted accordingly using the T&E. His final score, a 95 out of a possible 200, was not good enough for a marksmanship badge, although his score was about average for the machine gun platoons.

They progressed from the record 1,000-in. range to field firing where they put the theories they had learned to use. They practiced machine gun manipulation in the morning, ate their lunch out of mess kits, and in the afternoon sandbagged the guns and fired on targets from 200 out to 1,000 yds. Each man had to be sparing with his ammunition though, as only 100 rounds were available to each. The practice of firing short bursts on the 1,000-in. range paid rich dividends.

John learned to adjust moving the burst into the target. Using the T&E, he had to calculate how many clicks of traverse it took to move the strike of the round from the initial burst to the target. For example, when he fired on a target at 750 yds, he observed the strike 10 yds to the right and about 50 yds short of the target, so he would traverse the gun to the left 15 clicks (mils) and add one or more clicks (mils), depending on the slope. Once on target this was a great method to remain there, however it took some time adjusting to the target.

The technique John most liked, and was best at, was the adjusted aiming point method where he walked the rounds to the target by estimating the distance to the target from the strike of tracers and dust. For example, when he fired on a target at 500 yds and estimated that the rounds impacted 30 yds short and 15 yds to the right, he moved his aiming point about 30 yds beyond the target and 15 yds to its left and fired again, usually hitting the target with his second burst.

The last day of the month, unless it was a Sunday, was payday. Pay for a private was $21 a month, less allotments. John stood at parade rest near the end of the alphabetically ordered line, waiting his turn with the pay officer. When he was the next man to be paid, he rapped sharply on the door and waited for the word "Enter." He marched to within two steps of the pay table, halted, saluted, and said: "Sir, Private Smith reports for pay." The lieutenant looked him up and down, looked at his pay record, and counted out 11 crisp one-dollar bills. John had received the other $10 as a partial pay for incidentals when he first reported to Fort McPherson. John bent at the waist and scrawled his name on an entry line next to his name. He re-assumed the position of the soldier, stepped back one pace, halted, saluted, executed an about face, and left the room. Outside he passed a line of pay tables for the company fund, barber shop, war bonds, PX (Post Exchange), and other entities wanting soldiers' money.

Guard duty was also a fixture of John's training. Before guard mount, everyone prepared by memorizing the 11 General Orders as well as the names of the different commanders in the chain of command, and anything else they thought the officer of the guard would ask as he inspected the three files of guard shifts. Guard mount over, the men went to their anti-aircraft alert duty posts, where each sentinel pulled guard one in three: with two hours on, and four hours off.

Guard Duty General Orders

GENERAL ORDERS
1. To take charge of this post and all Government property in view.
2. To walk my post in a military manner, keeping always on the alert and observing everything that takes place within sight or hearing.
3. To report all violations of orders I am instructed to enforce.
4. To repeat all calls from posts more distant from the guardhouse than my own.
5. To quit my post only when properly relieved.
6. To receive, obey, and pass on to the sentinel who relieves me all orders from the commanding officer, officer of the day, and officers and noncommissioned officers of the guard only.
7. To talk to no one except in the line of duty.
8. To give the alarm in case of fire or disorder.
9. To call the corporal of the guard in any case not covered by instructions.
10. To salute all officers and all colors and standards not cased.
11. To be especially watchful at night and, during the time for challenging, to challenge all persons on or near my post and to allow no one to pass without proper authority.

One of the last experiences of his basic training was the Dismounted Full Field Inspection as portrayed on page 78 of the *Soldier's Handbook*. The entire battalion arrayed on the parade field and at the commands "Unsling equipment," "Display equipment" they lined up, covered off to the front and sides, pitched tents, and laid out equipment for display precisely as prescribed: mess kit knife with cutting edge to the right, gas mask with strap vertical, shaving brush with bristles down. When the inspecting officers began their inspection, the soldiers stood between their tents in ranks as straight and orderly as rows of corn. Inspection complete, a bugle sounded and the soldiers pulled out the tent pegs on the right side while holding the tents erect. At the next bugle call they folded the tents to the left in one mass motion: each platoon vied with the others to see which would be repacked first and ready to leave.

During the last day they turned in their bedding and working equipment but kept their gas masks and mess kits, which they packed among their other items in their two barracks bags. Officers and NCOs double-checked their equipment and their records before allowing them to supper, which was a celebration with pitchers of 3.2 beer on the tables. Later that night, orders came sending the newly minted infantrymen to different camps and divisions. In groups of 50 or so, including a lieutenant and a sergeant, the men boarded trains at the station throughout the night and next day.

REPLACEMENT

After several days of riding the train and sitting at sidings, John and his comrades arrived at Fort Meade, Maryland, where the 76th Infantry Division was forming. They had arrived just before the majority of the enlisted men who were coming straight from the reception stations and who were to take their basic training with the unit.

John immediately noticed the disorganization of the newly forming unit. There was too little equipment and most of the company officers and NCOs were newly promoted; many had only been in service since 1941. From what he could tell, there were four Regular Army (RA) NCOs and no RA officers in his company. He could tell the 76th was a low-priority unit by the equipment they trained with, much of which was older than the gear with which he had recently trained. They wore the old M1918A1 helmet and carried the old Springfield, as opposed to the new M1 helmet and M1 rifle, and machine guns were almost non-existent.

Since John was a trained soldier, his commander promoted him to private first class and made him a heavy machine gun squad leader, responsible for a seven-man squad although he continued to bunk in the same barracks they did. John had little idea of what to do, so he imitated the NCOs who had trained him as an infantryman: their standards and expectations had been clear. In the steadily forming 76th everyone was too new to have any experience to draw from. John noticed that field grade officers frequently inspected training, and that they often pulled the officers training the recruits to the side to confer with them, after which they usually changed the training, which didn't impress the soldiers they were trying to train.

John also noticed more "nickel and dime" infractions that his old instructors had corrected with an "ass chewing" or summary court-martial; here the same breaches saw soldiers digging 6ft × 6ft × 6ft pits, standing at attention and saluting passing officers for one or two hours, or cleaning steps with a toothbrush.

In September John heard that all the soldiers in the division were going to be shipped out as replacements, with more soldiers coming in to replace them. John felt his basic training had been adequate, but he knew that the training these soldiers had received in such a short time did not compare. They had not progressed very far with the weapons training because of the shortage of weapons, and those who were designated cooks, or mechanics got even less weapons training. Although they were infantrymen, they trained solely in their "specialty" almost as soon as they had arrived from the reception station. Other RTC graduates designated as replacements like John began arriving soon after.

John received a ten-day furlough home before shipping out in late October. It was not easy to hitchhike with gas rationing, but John made it home by train and bus in two days. He stayed for seven days saying good-byes, and then headed back to Fort Meade, arriving two days late. His thought at home was "What are they going to do, send me overseas?" Later, after demotion to private and a stay in the brig, he thought differently.

Pay for a private increased from $21 to $50 per month in September 1942. Anticipating combat, John signed up for $10,000 worth of the government's National Service Life Insurance at $6.40 per month and made out an allotment to his family for $30, figuring that he could live on just over $10 per month until he was promoted again.

After leaving Fort Meade, John and his comrades passed from one organization to another, with little time in any to get their bearings. Many were RTC graduates, but there were also some who had received all their training in the 76th or 78th Infantry Divisions.

Once at Camp Kilmer, New Jersey, John and his comrades underwent another medical screening, were issued a dismounted cartridge belt, a new M1 helmet, and pins and poles to go with the already issued shelter half, a gas mask, and a mess kit. Officers informed them the equipment they were missing would be issued once they arrived overseas. They boarded a darkened troop transport and filed into cramped holds with bunk beds stacked five high. Here they stayed for almost the entire voyage, except when they were standing in line for one of the two daily meals that they took standing up.

On arrival in Oran, Algiers, all of the replacements debarked and assisted in setting up tents in the replacement camp. Soldiers of every MOS imaginable bunked together. There was little to no training, and while the men waited for orders to the front they did little except serve as details unloading ships. Soon it was 1943 and, because of the battle of

Replacements wait to board a train. All of them carry the gas mask, some an M1936 Musette bag, and are dressed in various patterns of HBTs. It is summer, and some have partially rolled up their sleeves.

Kasserine Pass and other engagements, the demand for replacements at the front increased. John noticed that riflemen left first. By the time it was his turn, the camp consisted mostly of heavy weapons and infantry rear-echelon men (cooks, clerks, and mechanics).

One day in early March, the camp cadre assembled John along with hundreds of other soldiers. They were issued with M1 rifles, plus what little other equipment there was available to cover what had not been issued in the United States. Loaded in the back of open two-and-a-half-ton trucks, they were driven the several hundred miles to the front in Tunisia. John didn't realize just how cold North Africa was until they drove through some of the high mountain passes. He was happy finally to be going to a unit, but many of the soldiers in the truck with him were not infantrymen, and some told him they had never even fired their rifles.

NORTH AFRICA

Reception and Integration

John and his truckload arrived at their new regiment, the 133d Infantry of the 34th Infantry Division, during the last days of March 1943. Before shipping to a company, NCOs inspected their equipment, and each soldier was interviewed by the personnel section. The personnel clerk asked John what type of training he had, what weapons he had qualified with, and other pertinent questions.

Soldiers wait in foxholes, their M1 rifles at the ready. Those with helmets (one of whom is a Private First Class) have their chinstraps buckled, but the soldier in the background has opted for a woolen hat.

Since only a few of the replacements were riflemen, John found himself assigned to a rifle company in the 1st Battalion that had suffered heavy losses in the recapture of Kef-el-Amar Pass on March 11. Only six enlisted replacements besides John's shipment had arrived for the 133d since February 9, and every rifle company was short of men. When John complained that he was a heavy machine gunner, the personnel sergeant told him the heavy weapons companies were up to strength and that the rifle companies had priority on the replacements. Other heavy weapons soldiers, clerks, cooks, and mechanics also found themselves serving in rifle companies.

The men selected for the 1st Battalion loaded the trucks and headed for its companies guarding Sbeitla airport. At each stop the sergeant got out of the cab, walked to the back, and called surnames off his nearly alphabetical list. At John's company, the sergeant called out surnames from M through S, and then gave the list to the company first sergeant who assigned the men to the platoons. John found himself a rifleman in a rifle platoon. The first sergeant assured him however, that if he lived, and if there was an opening in the weapons platoon, and if the company received more replacements, he might later be assigned to the weapons platoon.

Infantrymen move forward. Each soldier has his raincoat and overcoat attached in a horseshoe roll around his M1928 haversack, and two canteens hang from each man's cartridge belt. Among the identifiable weapons are the M1 rifle and M1918A2 BAR.

John's next stop was his platoon leader, who assigned him to a squad after asking him when he had last qualified with his M1. He was surprised and angered when John told him he had only familiarized with it, and that more than six months ago. John didn't even know how to break the weapon down to clean it. During the next few days those unfamiliar with the M1 fired hundreds of rounds apiece at targets in the desert and practiced squad and platoon tactics. It was all the company could do to prepare them as riflemen.

John found that his regiment was a National Guard outfit from Idaho, overseas since February 1942, the same month he had entered service. They had landed from the UK in North Africa on January 3, 1943 and been in the front lines since the middle of February. About two-thirds were high school graduates and a third of them had attended college. His company commander appeared to be in his late thirties, as did many of the NCOs. The men in the company were friendly enough to the replacements, but they spent most of their time with one another, leaving the new men by themselves.

First Combat

On April 7, John's battalion moved forward toward Fondouk with the regiment's other battalion. He discovered one of the reasons his regiment was often held back in reserve and not on the front line was because its 2d Battalion was the "Palace Guard" for General Eisenhower's headquarters.

The hill masses of Fondouk loomed high over the desert sand, enabling the Germans to observe every move on the desert floor. John's regiment attacked at 0500hrs in column of companies, with his company last to move out of the protecting cover. Their objective was a hill barely discernable though the haze, about five miles away.

John followed as the next-to-last man in his squad of ten, two short of authorization. He felt more comfortable with his M1, but he was still unsure of what to do other than follow the leader. They advanced across a field of poppies by squad bounds. As they moved, the platoon leader picked out locations for the base squad to move to, with the remainder of the platoon following. With the haze burning off, the men felt the

Germans watching their every move. Just as they began crossing the wadi (a dry riverbed) that lay in their path, artillery, mortar, and then machine gun fire began landing among the soldiers. Everyone went to ground and tried to find even the smallest bit of cover.

When the company commander was wounded, John's platoon leader yelled to his platoon sergeant that he had assumed command of the company, and for the sergeant to take control of the platoon. The attack continued in fits and starts across the open desert. The men could see no one to shoot at; all they could do was move forward toward a cactus patch at the nose of their objective, hoping that it might offer some concealment from the German observers.

They were still advancing slowly when M3 Lee and the new M4 Sherman tanks of the 751st Tank Battalion drove through their lines. John felt a quick thrill as he watched the tanks move forward in clouds of dust. The German fire shifted from the infantry to the tanks, and soon tanks were burning on the desert floor; those not knocked out pulled back behind the helpless infantry.

The next day was much the same. Whenever they moved, German artillery and mortar fire rained down on the men. By the afternoon of April 9, one of the companies was near the road that ran diagonally across their front. The enemy fire was too intense to move much closer, and casualties were creeping higher.

After dusk fell, John's company followed the company ahead as it circled to the right behind the company near the road, and then John's company passed behind it, until the three companies were on line along the road. Word passed to the men to drop everything except their cartridge belts, bayonets, entrenching tools, water, and grenades, and prepare to attack that night. This way the German's would not see them until it was too late.

Word passed that John's company was to take the far right side of the hill. The highest point on the top of the hill was the dividing point between the companies, with the area on the left assigned to the left-most company, and the portion on the right assigned to the remaining two rifle companies. Weapons remained on safe, and orders were that they were not to fire unless fired upon.

The battalion attacked at 2200hrs, just as the waxing crescent moon dropped below the mountains to the right rear. With just the stars for light, John's company advanced on a compass bearing, in column of platoons, with soldiers within one or two yards of another. Every so often, someone kicked a rock; otherwise, it was deathly quiet. They passed quietly

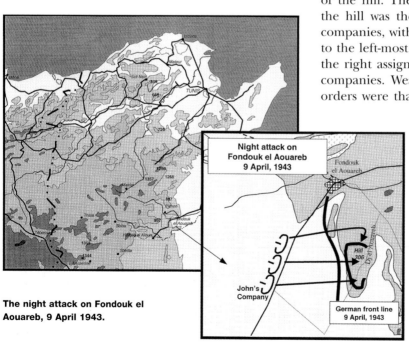

The night attack on Fondouk el Aouareb, 9 April 1943.

between what they believed were the German listening posts and began climbing the hill's steep slopes. John was sure the Germans could hear his heart beat. About three-quarters of the way up the slope, there was a whoosh as a green flare from one of the German positions on the hill shot into the air, illuminating John and his comrades. Machine guns and grenades quickly followed, but the Americans were too close; firefights began and ended at less than 10 yds. The gap in the German line widened as men still on the slope made it to the top and split off to the right and left, overrunning the enemy positions before them. John found himself on his company's left flank, with heavy firing from what he thought was another company off to his left. It was all confusion. Weapons-fire lit the sky like lightning. John instinctively fired at men wearing "coalscuttle" helmets highlighted in the muzzle flashes. Too many soldiers were randomly firing in the dark and rounds were going everywhere.

By 0100hrs, the battle was over, and leaders tried to find their soldiers in the pitch black to put together some semblance of a perimeter before the Germans launched a counterattack. But no attack came. After the battle, an intense fatigue washed over John, and it was all he could do to scratch a position in the hard earth; he kept nodding off while sitting up, awakening when his head bounced forward on his chest. The only way to stay awake was to work. It was the same in all the single-man foxholes.

Fondouk Pass fell the next day to the 133d in conjunction with the 135th Infantry and British tanks. Total casualties in John's company averaged 18 percent. Four of the five officers were wounded as were four NCOs and 16 other ranks. Only one soldier died during the two-day battle.

They stayed at Fondouk, training with tanks and artillery the next few days because the coordination between the infantry, tanks, and artillery was poor. John noticed that everyone was more attentive than they had been before the battalion's first big battle. Later, after returning to the Maktar area for rest and reconstitution, the men spent more time on night operations. All had a new respect for night attacks that allowed them to draw close to enemy positions, instead of trying to attack in the daylight when every move was watched.

Before the battle, officers and NCOs had removed their rank so they would not be ready targets for snipers. General George Patton visited the battalion at Maktar and found he couldn't tell the leaders from the privates, so he ordered the men to have their ranks pinned or sewn on by the next morning.

In late April John's regiment was again in the front lines for the 34th Division's assault against the fortified hill positions near Sidi Nsir. John's company was in

A patrol moves through a platoon position in Tunisia.

Hill 609.

reserve and played little part in the battalion's capture of Hill 609. John remembered more his reaction to the atabrine pills and the six-hour march in darkness to the jump-off point more than anything else.

In the rear areas, medics handed out a yellow pill known as atabrine to combat malaria. The pill itself was very bitter, and its prolonged use imparted a yellow hue to the skin. Its side effects were headaches, nausea, diarrhea, vomiting, and in some cases, temporary psychosis. The rumor quickly spread that the Army was issuing the pill to decrease their sex drive. What had not been determined was the amount of atabrine needed to combat malaria, so to be safe rather than sorry, medics issued soldiers larger doses than required.

Ordered to attack early the next morning, John's battalion began to move to its attack positions at 2130hrs the night of 29 April. His company began the march forward about 2200hrs after the battalion's other companies had moved out. As at Fondouk, the soldiers walked so close together in the darkness as to almost touch one another. They followed a narrow, rocky, and winding trail, part of it below the cliffs along the Sidi Nsir River. There were numerous breaks between the lead and trail elements when soldiers negotiating difficult parts of the trail halted the column behind them while those ahead kept walking. It was shuffle forward, stop; wait to cross the obstacle, cross; then hurry to catch up with the lead element. At the next obstacle, the process repeated itself.

John was unhappy that his company was last in order of movement, standing and waiting for the men ahead to move, marching two or three paces and then waiting again, all the while his bowels churning from the large dose of atabrine. He was not the only victim, as many of the men experienced acute attacks of diarrhea and nausea while moving to the assembly area.

Soldiers in training near Oran.

The nighttime movement ended at 0400hrs, and men fell asleep where they sat, while commanders reconnoitered and received the final assault orders. At 0515hrs, the assault companies moved forward with the tanks that had moved up during the early morning. John's company followed as reserve some 500 yds behind.

Unlike Fondouk, infantry and armor worked well together. John watched infantrymen walk alongside the tanks and point out targets for them to engage, while the infantrymen nearby protected the tanks. By 0645hrs, Hill 609 was won, and the soldiers began digging-in against German long-range artillery. Not a soldier in John's company was killed or wounded but other companies were not as fortunate.

After two days in position, John's battalion pulled back to an assembly area. For the next six days, John and his fellow soldiers walked the hills and mountains, clearing the

Training at Camp Wheeler, Georgia, March 1942: the 100 yd obstacle course

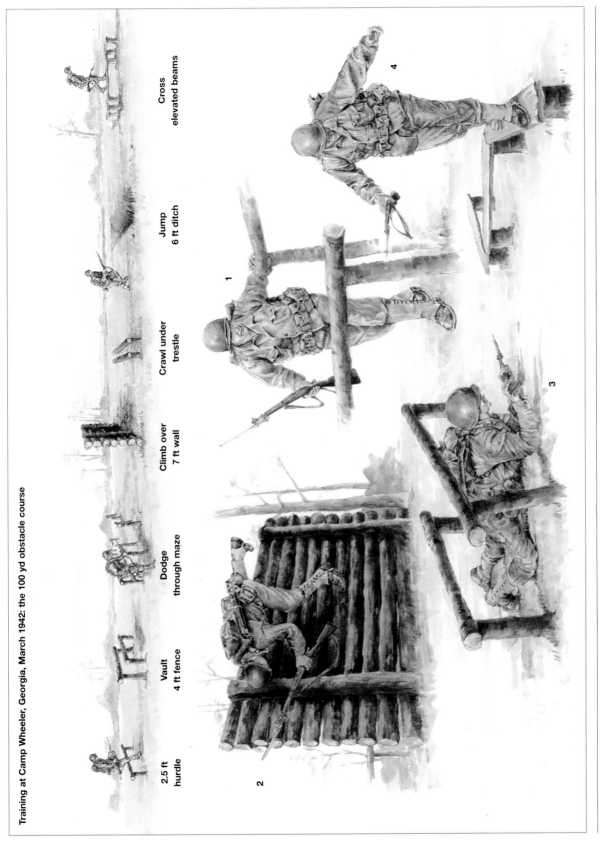

2.5 ft
hurdle

Vault
4 ft fence

Dodge
through maze

Climb over
7 ft wall

Crawl under
trestle

Jump
6 ft ditch

Cross
elevated beams

A

John as a Rifleman, 1st Battalion 133d Infantry Regiment, Tunisia, March 1943
(see plate commentary
for full details)

B

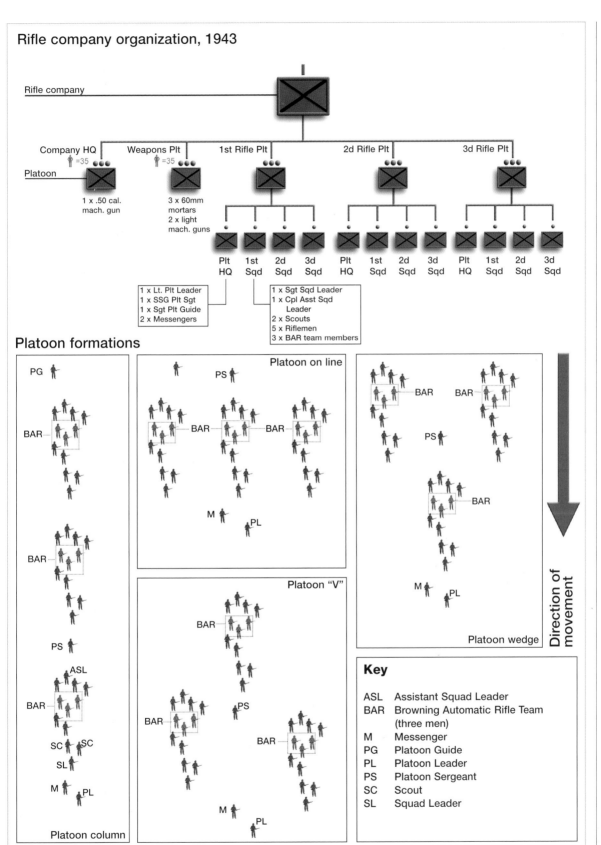

Rifle company organization, 1943

Rifle company

Company HQ — 👤 =35 ●●●
Platoon

1 x .50 cal. mach. gun

Weapons Plt — 👤 =35 ●●●

3 x 60mm mortars
2 x light mach. guns

1st Rifle Plt ●●●

2d Rifle Plt ●●●

3d Rifle Plt ●●●

Plt HQ | 1st Sqd | 2d Sqd | 3d Sqd
Plt HQ | 1st Sqd | 2d Sqd | 3d Sqd
Plt HQ | 1st Sqd | 2d Sqd | 3d Sqd

1 x Lt. Plt Leader
1 x SSG Plt Sgt
1 x Sgt Plt Guide
2 x Messengers

1 x Sgt Sqd Leader
1 x Cpl Asst Sqd Leader
2 x Scouts
5 x Riflemen
3 x BAR team members

Platoon formations

Platoon column

PG
BAR
BAR
PS
ASL
BAR
SC   SC
SL
M   PL

Platoon on line

PS
BAR   BAR
M   PL

Platoon "V"

BAR
BAR   PS
BAR
M   PL

Platoon wedge

BAR   BAR
PS
BAR
M   PL

Direction of movement

Key

ASL	Assistant Squad Leader
BAR	Browning Automatic Rifle Team (three men)
M	Messenger
PG	Platoon Guide
PL	Platoon Leader
PS	Platoon Sergeant
SC	Scout
SL	Squad Leader

c

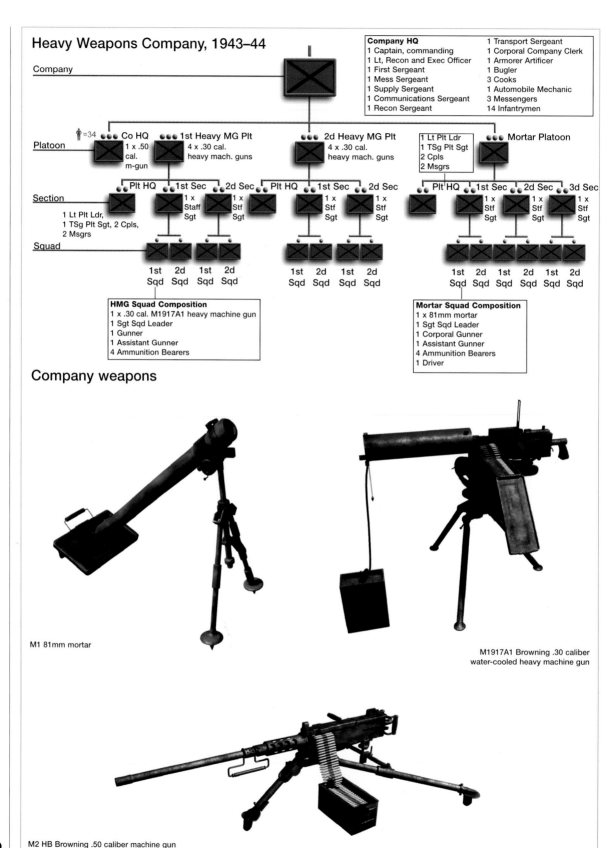

Heavy Weapons Company, 1943–44

Company HQ
- 1 Captain, commanding
- 1 Lt, Recon and Exec Officer
- 1 First Sergeant
- 1 Mess Sergeant
- 1 Supply Sergeant
- 1 Communications Sergeant
- 1 Recon Sergeant
- 1 Transport Sergeant
- 1 Corporal Company Clerk
- 1 Armorer Artificer
- 1 Bugler
- 3 Cooks
- 1 Automobile Mechanic
- 3 Messengers
- 14 Infantrymen

Company

Platoon

♟ = 34

Co HQ
1 x .50 cal. m-gun

1st Heavy MG Plt
4 x .30 cal. heavy mach. guns

2d Heavy MG Plt
4 x .30 cal. heavy mach. guns

Mortar Platoon
1 Lt Plt Ldr
1 TSg Plt Sgt
2 Cpls
2 Msgrs

Section

1 Lt Plt Ldr, 1 TSg Plt Sgt, 2 Cpls, 2 Msgrs

Plt HQ

1st Sec — 1 x Staff Sgt

2d Sec — 1 x Stf Sgt

Plt HQ

1st Sec — 1 x Stf Sgt

2d Sec — 1 x Stf Sgt

Plt HQ

1st Sec — 1 x Stf Sgt

2d Sec — 1 x Stf Sgt

3d Sec — 1 x Stf Sgt

Squad

1st Sqd 2d Sqd 1st Sqd 2d Sqd

1st Sqd 2d Sqd 1st Sqd 2d Sqd

1st Sqd 2d Sqd 1st Sqd 2d Sqd 1st Sqd 2d Sqd

HMG Squad Composition
- 1 x .30 cal. M1917A1 heavy machine gun
- 1 Sgt Sqd Leader
- 1 Gunner
- 1 Assistant Gunner
- 4 Ammunition Bearers

Mortar Squad Composition
- 1 x 81mm mortar
- 1 Sgt Sqd Leader
- 1 Corporal Gunner
- 1 Assistant Gunner
- 4 Ammunition Bearers
- 1 Driver

Company weapons

M1 81mm mortar

M1917A1 Browning .30 caliber water-cooled heavy machine gun

M2 HB Browning .50 caliber machine gun

Heavy weapons positions

Spoil is piled around and camouflaged, forming a low parapet

c.1.5 feet

TOP VIEW

c.6 feet

Gun platform

c.3 feet

M1917A1 heavy machine gun position

Greenery used for camouflage

M1 81mm mortar postion

line of sight

c.4 feet

Ammunition shelter

Assistant Gunner's position

c.6 feet

Gunner's position

c.5 feet

TOP VIEW

65 mils

65 mils

Maximum traverse

E

F

Monte Cassino house clearing, 1944

1. M4A2 Sherman tank blasts house at close range

2. First group of infantrymen move from cover, and toss grenades through ground floor door and windows

3. Supporting troops launch rifle grenades into top floor, and watch for German soldiers

4. Enemy occupiers surrender: second group of infantry and the tank move on to the next house

60mm mortar squad

10

9

8

7 (traverse)
70 mils
70 mils

6 (elevation)
85°
40°

G

John, Staff Sergeant, Italy, early 1945

Eddekhila and Chougui Passes. On the morning of May 8, word passed that, for the 34th Infantry Division, the war in North Africa was over

For the next three months the men policed the battlefields of German and Allied equipment, building and running staging areas for divisions preparing for the invasion of Sicily. In August, they returned to the Oran area for mountain training and the Fifth Army Battle School, where they participated in extremely realistic live fire exercises; several men were killed or wounded in the training.

In early September John and his comrades received word to begin packing for overseas movement. With Sicily fallen, there was only one destination: Italy. The 100th (Nisei) Battalion joined the 133d Regiment as its 2d Battalion for the coming operation. John and his comrades wondered how this new battalion would fight.

ITALY 1943–44, SALERNO TO CASSINO

With the attached 100th (Nisei) Battalion in place of the regiment's 2d Battalion, the 133d Infantry numbered 3,981 men, almost 600 over its authorized strength when it landed on September 22. The 1,432-man Nisei Battalion was almost as large as two standard infantry battalions, and was organized around five rifle companies (A–E), with heavy weapons, service, and headquarters companies. All the enlisted men were Nisei (Americans of Japanese descent), and the battalion could not draw replacements from the normal pool. It was not until after the bloodletting at Cassino that replacements arrived from the United States. In the interim, as casualties ate away at rifle company strength, the five companies became three, and by February 1944, battalion strength stood at 521.

On September 22, 1943, when assault craft landed the 133d Infantry under fire at Salerno, Italy, John was no longer a "rookie". There was still much for him and the other members of his company to learn about the art of soldiering, however. He and the other replacements were still a minority in the company, most members having come overseas with it.

Soldiers of the 34th Infantry Division move through an Italian town. The two men to the fore carry the M1903 Springfield sniper rifle and the others the M1 rifle. The man on the left carries what appears to be his raincoat folded over his cartridge belt. They have the "Red Bull" stenciled on their helmets.

During the following six weeks, John's 133d Infantry Regiment fought up through the rough, mountainous terrain to its first real action near Benevento, across the Calore River and up to make their first crossing of the Volturno River, learning as it went. A second nighttime crossing of the river brought them out on to open terrain near San Angelo D'Alife, and then they crossed the Volturno a third time: they never seemed to dry out.

During the early days of the campaign, much learning occurred. Although John and his comrades had seen combat, many of the lessons in the books were relearned the hard way.

One of the quickly validated lessons from the field manuals was the use of binoculars and observation positions. After entering a town, John's sergeant climbed to the second story in a building to observe the terrain in front. Instead of remaining in the shade and away from the window, he became too interested in observing and moved close to the window opening. A sniper saw the glint from his binoculars and shot him. John, now the most senior man, acted as squad leader until they left the line.

Later they moved into a quiet sector. Since their position was visible to the Germans, they kept everything under cover. After about a week, a soldier hung a towel and his underwear out the window to dry: the result was an enemy barrage, casualties, and a now active sector.

Soldiers clear an Italian farmhouse of snipers. Several men watch the windows, while others approach the house from its blind side.

John and his comrades found that the Germans were fond of planting mines, and they were almost more afraid of them than facing machine guns. They also noticed the Germans were very neat. In some of the fully marked minefields that the Germans had left with signs and wire, tall clover grew over buried mines, and in the mine-free lanes, the grass was mowed.

After a night attack that completely surprised the Germans, John's company dug in, and prepared for the coming day. At first light, a single German, about 300 yds distant, jumped up and ran back toward his lines. One rifleman fired and missed, then another and another. Soon everyone was firing at the moving target, giving away the company positions. What seemed like the whole German army responded with heavy small arms and artillery fire, killing or wounding many in the company and forcing John's comrades deep into their holes for the remainder of the day. Another lesson learned.

It was fall; a chill was in the air and the water cold as the men fought their way up Italy's "boot" through grape arbors and villages until they reached the lower range of the Volturno River and crossed it again.

Night Attack across the Volturno

John walked down the chow line with his helmet in one hand and mess kit in the other. The mess sergeant put five K rations and a D ration bar in the helmet, while the cook's helpers filled his mess kit with a steaming stew of meat and potatoes. After chow, platoon sergeants sent details to draw ammunition from the supply sergeant: a bandoleer of 96 rounds for each rifleman, 500 rounds for each BAR, two grenades a man, rounds for the carbines, and signaling flares. Now extremely practiced, John rolled his blanket into his shelter half and attached the roll to his haversack in almost total darkness, knowing instinctively where every strap was. Then it began raining and John sought shelter under some low bushes, keeping his haversack on his shoulders as a backrest and leaning into it. His head soon rested on his chest, eyes closed, while the rain dripped on his helmet.

Sometime later he awoke, shivering and stiff. The night was pitch black with low cloud overhead. Soldiers around him were stirring and standing. One of his buddies helped pull him to his feet and he did the same for the man next to him. The column wound its way up the muddy trail, with men sliding or falling at almost every step.

John followed the dirty piece of white engineer tape tied to the haversack of the man in front. It was a lesson learned some time back that helped prevent men from losing contact with one another while walking in the darkness. It also told John what was up ahead: if the tape went down, the man in front had stepped in a hole; up and the man was climbing; down fast meant he was on a slope and if it slid sideways it meant the man was sliding down the slope. Whenever someone slipped, the line behind him waited while he got back up, but the line in front kept moving forward, threatening to leave the waiting men in the rear. It was almost midnight when the company reached the attack position, and the men began digging hasty positions in the mud.

When it was time to move, the soldiers formed in squad columns with men dispersed just far enough apart that they had the next man in sight. The communications man walking with the commander had a roll of assault telephone wire that he paid out as they shuffled forward. The commander had radios also, but chances were they wouldn't be functioning when they arrived at the other side. At 2400hrs the artillery started and the soldiers crossed the river. Once on the other side, they assumed attack formation.

John's company led the assault with his platoon third in line. The lead platoon angled right toward an orchard to conceal their movement. Not long after entering, John heard a series of blasts followed by screams and then silence. Someone had detonated a series of mines, wounding the platoon leader and all the NCOs. The eight men remaining in the lead platoon walked back along the formation and fell in behind the trailing platoon. The second platoon in line then took the lead, veering to the left of the orchard. Another series of explosions, whispers for a medic passing the word that the lieutenant and some others were down and needed help. Now it was the third platoon's turn to lead. John's squad followed their platoon leader as he backtracked a section and steered a large arc around the mined areas. They walked in the dark for about an hour when with a flash and crack, an explosion blew the lieutenant into the air, and injured those directly behind him. Those not wounded stood still, hearts beating, not wanting to put a foot wrong. They heard the company commander moving forward to see what was going on when another blast killed the commander and wounded still more. As his squad leader was wounded, John took command and had his men begin probing for mines with their bayonets while they slowly turned around and retraced their steps to safety. With all the officers down as well as several of the enlisted men – mainly NCOs – John's company fell back to the rear of the battalion to become the reserve, while another company took the lead.

No longer up in front, John and his comrades listened as more mines exploded. They'd been walking almost five hours as dawn colored the sky, when they heard German machine gun fire to their front. Everyone heaved a collective sigh of relief because they knew then that they had cleared the mined area. John, along with his comrades, knew that the only place sure not to be mined was the

A soldier removes a German "Bouncing Betty" S-mine with an M1918 "knuckle buster" trench knife. Once triggered, and after a slight pause, an ejector charge blew the mine into the air where it exploded, sending hundreds of small steel balls out to a radius of about five yards.

enemy position, so they surged forward through machine gun and mortar fire to seize the objective.

Winter 1943

During the winter months of 1943, John's regiment held its forward positions in the same manner as the Germans. Only a few soldiers occupied positions on the forward slope, while support positions were located on the reverse slope, out of enemy sight. Battalions rotated up and down the mountains to provide short intervals of rest, although they provided the carrying parties for the men on top. The constant rain turned the dirt roads to quagmires and the ever-present fog hid the mountain peaks from the valleys. Once wet, nothing dried without fire, and there was no fire in the forward positions. On the reverse side of the hill, John and his comrades searched for dry leaves, straw, long grass or cardboard to put some distance between them and the cold ground. One man placed his blanket on top the long grass to keep at least some of the cold from penetrating and they used John's blanket as a cover.

Mules carried supplies up the winding trails as far as they could into the mountains. When the trails became too treacherous, men took over and back-packed the supplies the remaining two miles. Soldiers from battalions in reserve climbed the mountain every night, packing on average 85 five-gallon cans of water each weighing 40 lbs; 100 cardboard cases containing 12 K rations of three meals each and weighing about 44 lbs; 10 cases of 100 D ration bars (four-ounce bars of 600 calories each); 10 miles of telephone wire, 25 cases of grenades, plus rifle and machine-gun ammunition, about 100 81-mm mortar rounds, one radio, two telephones, and four cases of first aid packets and sulfa drugs. The back-packers also brought mail, additional cigarettes, and cans of Sterno so the men on top could heat coffee.

Ernie Pyle in *Brave Men* noted one 5ft 7in. 135 lb 18-year-old back-packer who made four trips to the top of a mountain in one day. Each trip took an unencumbered walker three hours; yet his climbs were with heavy load.

On one occasion, John and his comrades were relieved from their position and, as they hobbled down the trail, were stopped and pressed into service as guides along the trail because there was no one else to do it. Finally relieved, it took John almost an entire day to climb down the rest of the mountain because he could hardly walk. His feet swelled as soon as his wet boots and socks came off: they were mottled and numb. He'd gone almost two weeks without taking his boots off, leaving the laces loose for circulation. He massaged his feet and as they thawed, John felt first a tingling pain, then burning pain, and finally an intense itching. However, they did not discolor, and John was back for duty, and back up the mountain, within a week.

Sometime in November, the men packing supplies up the mountain arrived with heavy winter combat trousers and jackets to augment the HBTs, trench coats, and long underwear the men had been wearing. They also brought up cellophane gas capes,

Soldiers carry a litter patient down a steep slope.

normally used to protect against blister gases, from which the men fashioned impromptu sleeping covers.

One of the officers brought up a translation of an article, published in *Die Suedfront*, a German magazine for soldiers fighting in southern Italy that described American infiltration tactics of 1943:

> The Americans use quasi-Indian tactics. They search for the boundary lines between battalions or regiments, they look for gaps between our strongpoints, they look for the steepest mountain passages (guided by treacherous civilians … They infiltrate through these passages with a patrol, a platoon at first, mostly at dusk. At night, they reinforce the infiltrated units, and in the morning they are often in the rear of a German unit, which is being attacked from behind, or also from the flanks simultaneously.

The battalion was scattered across a series of pinnacles at about the 2,700ft level. It was always freezing or nearly so, and the water froze nightly in canteen necks. Supplies had to be hauled great distances over rough terrain by mule trains and carrying parties. It took litter bearers 12 hours to make a three-mile round trip carrying a single patient. During the winter months the Germans on the next mountain over were of secondary importance: they were probably suffering as much as John and his comrades. There were no truces and patrols still went out, but other than that it was "live and let live"; unless the other side became too complacent and walked around in the open on the forward slope.

Finally, after what seemed a lifetime of cold, the 133d Infantry pulled back to a rest area near Alife, Italy, for almost three weeks. John and his comrades took their first hot showers in months, exchanged their grimy and torn uniforms, cleaned equipment, and trained the many new replacements who were arriving. After about ten days of slacking, training began again, emphasizing physical hardening with marches, scouting, and patrolling. The marches were nothing for John and others who had spent much of their recent time hauling rations and ammunition up steep mountain trails. However, some soldiers discovered they'd been marching with collapsed arches or other lameness. In the warm, stress-free environment many men discovered they had been living with arthritis, hernia, or heart problems up on the mountain. All it took was less stress and proper rest for their bodies to signal they were broken. Some spent time in hospital and returned; others went back home to the United States.

Cassino

They moved forward again early in January 1944, taking hills leading to the Rapido River, crossing it on the night of January 24, in an effort to seize Cassino. John remembered little of the three weeks that followed.

One man called it a "little Stalingrad", with back and forth, see-saw, close-range house-to-house fighting. Tanks trundling down blocked and rubbled streets with infantry on both sides,

Soldiers fire an 81mm mortar into Cassino. The soldier on the left is the gunner, who sets the elevation and deflection on the mortar and keeps the bubbles on the sight level. The next man over is the assistant gunner, the next an ammunition bearer, and the man on the right is the mortar squad leader.

advancing until the tanks ran out of ammunition or were destroyed, and the infantry pushed back. The constant cold and wet, the tiredness from continual shaking and ever-present fear, only getting catnaps for sleep, watching friends be killed or wounded, and wondering who was next: it was debilitating and demoralizing.

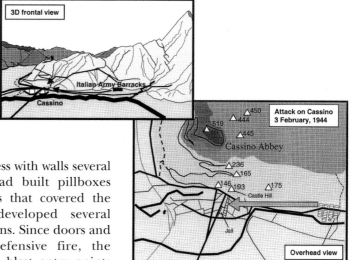

The attack on Cassino.

Each of the Italian houses was a fortress with walls several feet thick. In some, the Germans had built pillboxes containing antitank and machine guns that covered the critical intersections. John's unit developed several techniques to reduce the German positions. Since doors and windows were usually covered by defensive fire, the infantrymen used tanks or bazookas to blast entry points through walls. They found the pillboxes took fewer rounds to penetrate than the houses. When available, they used 8-in. howitzers to fire directly into the houses.

One afternoon in early February, about the tenth day of the battle, John's company, supported by a platoon of tanks, attacked into the smoke-blanketed northern sector of Cassino proper. A squad walked in front of the lead tank, the remaining two squads of the platoon behind. The company headquarters followed the second tank, one platoon the third tank, and John's platoon split into two groups; John's squad with the platoon headquarters following the fourth tank, while the remaining two squads brought up the rear. The company stood at fewer than 80 men, the preceding ten days of combat having sapped almost half the company's strength through both battle and nonbattle casualties.

A position built of rocks in the Cassino area.

Once they reached the outlying buildings, most two stories high, John watched as the lead elements began clearing each house individually, five or six men working against each. First a tank fired into the house, creating smoke, dust, and suppressing those inside; after which three men rushed forward, tossed in a grenade, waited for the blast, and then rushed through the door. The covering group fired rifle grenades through the upper windows, driving any Germans on the second floor down the stairs to be killed or captured by the men inside.

Then the next group would leapfrog the first and repeat the process. Two men remained in each cleared house to ensure the Germans did not reoccupy and the remainder continued down the street with the tanks.

As the band reached the first crossroad, a hidden antitank gun knocked out the third tank in the column while machine gun fire drove the remaining infantrymen into the doorways of houses alongside the street. The two leading tanks

couldn't pull back past the burning tank, so they stayed and fired their cannon and machine guns at every doorway and window nearby. John, his company commander, and about five other infantrymen rushed across a small square and seized two big buildings. They spent the rest of the night holding the buildings, waiting for reinforcements. Unfortunately, during the night, the two tanks found a way around the disabled third, and pulled back. With no radio communications, the commander relied on runners to get through to battalion: but none ever returned. When the sun rose in the morning, and with no relief in sight, he pulled the company back out of the town, picking up the riflemen who had remained in each house as they retreated. John wished that support had come, as he hated seeing good men wasted in a successful attack that had to be abandoned.

During the third week of February there wasn't much forward movement. John's company had captured the jail sometime during the second week, and had held on, too exhausted and too battered by the German fire to do more than await relief. Some of the fights had degenerated to rock throwing after both sides had run out of grenades, playing toss between houses just 10 yds apart.

The combat infantryman in Italy.

Unable to dig in the frozen ground, John and his comrades resorted to piling rubble around them for protection. The cold, wet weather caused more casualties than the Germans did, with trench foot and respiratory diseases affecting almost everyone. The only replacements to make it to the front lines were men from headquarters, motor pools, and kitchens. Soldiers remained pinned in these positions during the day because of the closeness of the enemy, and didn't move at night lest they be caught in the open by German shelling.

A general from outside the division visited once, and received an earful from officers and enlisted men alike on how the battle was progressing. When General Lemnitzer returned to 15th Army Group, he said the men around Cassino were dispirited and almost mutinous, and he recommended they be pulled out of the line for rest.

In the three weeks between its first attack to take the Italian barracks area and the final effort in the northeastern corner of Cassino, the 133d Infantry had captured 138 prisoners but had 132 killed, 492 wounded, and 115 missing; most were lost from rifle companies. Nonbattle casualties probably reached over 1,000, again primarily in the companies on the front lines. John's rifle company, like most of the others, averaged fewer than 50 men present when they pulled off the line.

The Nature of Combat

Combat against the Germans was not continuous: the infantryman's primal living conditions were. The constant rain and mud and never drying out; the unforgiving hard ground; the cold, almost indigestible, rations; everyone bearded and gray; the dirty, almost rotting feet, and unwashed bodies were combined with the unceasing movement forward, never catching up on the missed sleep of night movement or guard and patrolling. Men passed the point of being tired, and went on only because there was nothing else they could do. Days merged into other days, until dates and days didn't matter. Specific instances are remembered, but not within any context: "Do you remember...?" "Oh yes, that was the day Sam was killed." Emotions were hidden from all but the closest of friends, and when the friends were gone, feelings were locked away.

On the front line, there was a reduced military formality, with little difference between officers and men. The social divide was between veterans and replacements; in the rear areas it was different – it became again officer and enlisted men.

Only eight men of the original company that sailed from England in 1942, and about six, including John, who had arrived in Tunisia remained after Cassino. The brothers, uncles, and cousins who made up the old Guard company were gone: some killed, some captured, and others sent home, either invalided or rotated back. To some it seemed they had always been, and always would be, soldiers. They were all hard and wise in the animal ways of keeping themselves alive and knew they had survived initial combat only because they were lucky. They all wanted to go home, but they had been at it so long that they knew how to take care of themselves and how to lead others. Every company was built around these little cadres of veterans. By now, most of the men in John's rifle company, as in all the other rifle companies in his regiment, were replacements. Some had just arrived and some like John had been there so long that they were just as wizened as the original eight, with little noticeable difference between them.

Anzio

After Cassino, John and his comrades spent a month resting, reorganizing, and receiving replacements near Alife. The 2d Battalion returned from its 18-month tour as "palace guards." Unlike the companies in John's battalion, almost three-quarters of each company had been together since Northern Ireland, with very few replacements. It was an interesting contrast with the other battalions within the regiment. Two battalions had suffered through nine months of combat: their companies contained, on average, eight to 15 men who had landed in Tunisia; the rest were replacements, and all the survivors were sick of war. The other, at full strength, had yet to see combat: while the men were probably not eager for combat, they did want to prove themselves to the men of the other battalions.

The new replacements that arrived from the United States in 1944 had received different training to John. Their training was four weeks longer, included more field time, more time on the ranges firing their weapons, and almost unlimited ammunition. However, the cen-

The overseas shipment of infantry replacements to the Mediterranean Theater of Operations.

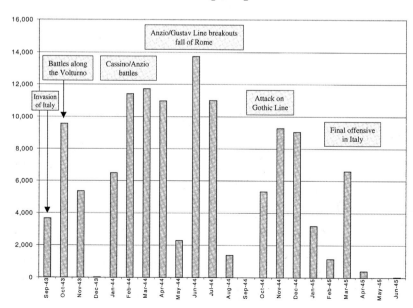

ters weren't teaching the intricacies of the trade. Most replacements hadn't the slightest idea of what a rifle sounded like to a man shot at and missed, or the "crack and thump" method of target detection. A soldier would hear the crack of the round overhead, and then the thump of the firearm's discharge. The two pointed an invisible arrow toward the shooter's position. By multiplying the number of seconds between the crack and the thump by 360 ft, (the distance sound travels in one second at 50 degrees), a soldier could determine the approximate range to the firer. The lower the temperature, the nearer the target; the higher the temperature, the farther away. Moreover, it seemed dumb for the replacements to learn the sounds of the different German weapons by being shot at.

The new replacements were concerned with the coming battle that would break the Allies out of Anzio and they listened very closely not only to their training but also to the old-timers' war stories. The newly arrived regiment's as yet unbloodied 2d Battalion listened just as closely.

To augment their near range firepower, the veterans advised the replacement soldiers preparing to clear a town to trade their rifles for tankers' submachine guns, then trade back after the action. They also advised welding two 30-round M3 "grease gun" submachine gun magazines together, one up and one down, so that all they had to do to keep firing was to eject the empty magazine, reverse it, insert it, and fire again. The only problem was that the magazine pointed down tended to foul with dirt. Those listening also noticed that many of the veterans had paid Italian shoemakers to sew a leather extension band that fastened with a buckle attachment around the tops of their combat boots. These boots were very similar to those worn by British "Tommies," and similar to the M1943 combat boot just arriving in theater.

John's regiment arrived at Anzio beachhead in late March, in the midst of a giant cloud of thick, oily, pale gray smoke, continually dispersed by hundreds of smoke generators. In mid-April they moved forward to defensive positions along the Mussolini Canal and the Cisterna River.

While in the defense, every company received heavy augmentation in machine guns, 74 light and 53 heavy guns being added to the regiment's normal authorization of 18 light and 24 heavies. It appeared that almost every position had some type of automatic weapon.

Infantrymen fighting from a destroyed building. The soldier on the left is firing a BAR.

John touched a heavy machine gun for the first time since leaving the States and spent the next few days remembering the intricacies of the weapon then training soldiers in his platoon, and later company, in its use. His commander, impressed with this unknown machine gunner, fulfilled the departed first sergeant's promise of a year ago in Tunisia, and assigned John to the company's light machine gun section. John turned in his M1 rifle for an M1911 pistol and an M1919A4 air-cooled machine gun. He found the tripods different between the heavy and light machine guns, but the technique and theory were the same.

An elderly Italian watches as American infantrymen move forward. The infantrymen no longer carry the M1928 haversacks: in their place are rolls more reminiscent of the American Civil War. This image also shows the men wearing the new M1943 combat boot.

A rifleman armed with an M1 rifle and scope watches over infantrymen as they move toward a house in a valley.

They dug two-man positions under the near side of the road passing through their sector; the heavy layers of asphalt provided excellent overhead cover from artillery and mortar fire. Those unfortunates who lacked such luxurious accommodation covered their abodes with ammunition boxes filled with sand, perforated steel planking, fence rails, and anything else that provided some support for the foot or so of dirt they piled on top. Usually there wasn't much artillery fire to speak of so John and his crew led a very quiet, inactive life. They even had hot rations or 10-and-1s (packaged rations suitable for ten men) instead of K and D rations.

One man per position stayed awake while the other slept at night. Both Germans and Americans infiltrated patrols into each other's rear areas to capture prisoners and gain information. One night while on guard, John saw a shadow walking toward the platoon's position. He waited until it got within challenging distance and softly called out, "Red," expecting "Rover" in reply. Nothing. He called out "Red" again, waited a few seconds and then fired his borrowed M1. A man fell. Alerted, several men from the different foxholes moved to check the body, and then looked up at John. He had killed a new replacement who had become disoriented in the dark, and frozen when asked the password. Although his comrades consoled him John felt terrible, but there was nothing else he could have done: he knew that it might have been a German.

The replacement was one of a group attached to the company for "battle inoculation." Normally during the Italian campaign, replacements arrived at units when they were out of the line. Just before the Anzio breakout, the 133d received 250 replacements to train in anticipation of predicted losses. Each battalion received about 80 men each, and John's company about 25. All would return to the newly formed regimental replacement company. This means of replacement continued in the 34th Division until the end of the war. Since this company was not TO&E, its cadre was drawn from the regiment's different companies, drawing down company strengths, but providing a safe haven for battle-weary veterans nearing exhaustion.

Machine Gunner

At 0630hrs on May 23, 1944, the Anzio Offensive began. The US/Canadian 1st Special Service Force passed through the positions held by John's regiment. Later that day his battalion moved forward, with his company capturing Highway 7 and on May 26, they attacked for three days toward Lanuvio.

On the move forward John located, by sound and observation, a German machine gun that had a rifle platoon pinned down. His team watched the position until the Germans

shifted to fire in a different direction. They quickly moved their gun to a good firing position, set it up, and John, using burst on target, walked the rounds over the gun crew and silenced the gun. Mission accomplished, they pulled back under cover. Later the same day, a German counterattack struck John's company while it was crossing another field. Instead of immediately engaging the Germans, John waited until most were in the field, and then began firing at those behind the leading echelons as if he were hunting turkeys. The fire demoralized the lead elements: cut off from support, he watched them first stop, then go to ground.

His machine gun crew's luck did not last. A German patrol surprised John and his crew as they supported his company's advance across a wheat field. His assistant gunner died almost immediately, and his ammunition bearers retreated over the hill.

Unable to bring his machine gun to bear, John lay flat on his stomach just under a hail of bullets. Every time he moved, a bit of him popped above his cover and provoked more firing. Knowing a grenade would soon be coming his way, he broke for the rear, but he was knocked to the ground by a blow to his chest. Every breath he took sucked air into the wound, threatening to collapse a lung, and causing him intense pain. John formed a seal by putting his hand over the bloody hole, and almost instantly felt his chest recompress; and although breathing was still painful, it was easier. He rolled over on his stomach to keep his hand pressed against the wound if he passed out, and hoped that help would soon come.

WOUNDED, RECOVERY AND RETURN

John fainted as soon as he saw helmets painted front and back with a red cross. He awoke in the division clearing station (see Warrior 45 *US Infantryman in World War II (1) Pacific Area of Operations 1941–45* for a discussion of casualty processing from battlefield to collecting station.)

The clearing station functioned as a small hospital. Above Anzio, the roads were relatively good and the clearing stations were close behind the regiments they supported.

An ambulance holding four litter patients brought John in from the 133d's collecting company. The dirt, shock, and exhaustion on every casualty's face made them all look the same. As medics removed the men from the vehicle, they sorted them by severity of injury. The seriously wounded, who needed lifesaving care were treated immediately, while those in less critical condition waited, and those who did not need immediate assistance were shipped without further care to a hospital further back. Those who were beyond help were set aside and made comfortable until they died.

With his sucking chest wound, John was treated as one of the seriously wounded – one who was expected to live with treatment. Had he been less severely wounded, his injuries would

An M17A1 Browning water-cooled machine gun concealed in the trees.

have been dressed and rebandaged at the clearing station, and he would have been moved to an evacuation hospital for surgery.

A hospital platoon set up next to the clearing station removed the 9mm machine pistol bullet from John's chest. While waiting to be operated on, John lay in a central holding area, in a corner of which lay men with thin white gauze over their faces – dying men. One could only tell they were alive by the flutter of their breath on the gauze. The chaplain passed among them, performing last rites, leading those who were semi-conscious through prayers.

John had been given one ampoule of morphine and was sleeping when time came for his surgery. His litter was his operating table: two medics lifted it up and laid it across two large trunks. After the operation was over, more medics took John to a post-operative tent. When he had

Medics load a wounded soldier onto a jeep that is fixed with welded brackets to accept stretchers. The two soldiers to the right both have entrenching tools attached to their web gear. The medics are clearly identifiable by the large Red Cross symbols on their helmets.

With the ground too hard to dig, infantrymen resorted to blowing holes in the ice and rock with satchel charges. Additional spade work turned the holes into fighting positions for front-line infantry.

recovered sufficiently to move, he was shipped to a field hospital at Anzio proper to regain his strength. Within a week, he loaded onto an LST for shipment to a convalescent hospital near Naples.

The convalescent hospital was a place where men who no longer needed constant medical or surgical care, but had not yet recovered, could rest and recuperate. Those whose expected recovery was longer than the theater's evacuation policy transferred to a hospital in the United States (between 1943 and 1945, evacuation policy to the United States varied between 30 and 120 days). The shorter the stay, the more bed spaces were freed for coming casualties, but the fewer men available in theater to go back to their units upon recovery.

John didn't consider his wound a misfortune, but a blessing. He was happy that he was alive and not too seriously wounded; although his friends were still up on the front line, he was glad he wasn't there. He had volunteered to fight but he also felt he had paid his dues and it was now his turn to sleep on clean white sheets, look at pretty nurses, eat good food, and be able to wash regularly. He also hoped that his wound might get him home, or at least out of combat. In September, John was discharged from the convalescent hospital and reassigned to a conditioning company near Rome that prepared men mentally and physically to re-enter combat.

Many of the men returning for combat duty were battle fatigue (neuropsychiatric) cases. In Italy during 1943 and 1944, these cases ranged between 1,200 and 1,500 per year per 1,000-man strength in many rifle battalions. As the war progressed, more veteran officers and NCOs with extended time on the front lines fell victim to neuroses. One psychiatrist estimated that infantrymen had an aggregate of 200–240 days on the line before cracking up – and the number of men on duty after this period was small and of negligible value. Many men, once diagnosed with battle fatigue, spent the rest of their time in the war shuffling between unit and hospital.

The men lived in prefabricated huts and went through a month of intensive training and marching, supplemented by organized athletics. The commandant frequently held parades and awards ceremonies to develop pride and raise the men's morale. During one of these ceremonies, John received the Bronze Star for his performance outside Lanuvio.

A winter patrol: soldiers dressed in cold weather parkas and camouflaged white helmets walk along a well-worn route.

Life on the reverse slope. Here things were easier, with positions dug into the earth and buttressed by sandbags. These warrens soon turned into reasonably warm abodes after the occupants spread cardboard and other materials on the ground, and the soldiers huddled close on top of four blankets, with four more on top them.

John remained in the conditioning unit about four weeks. He trained for the first three weeks, and spent the additional week in the depot receiving company. Here, a board of officers, including the company surgeon, interviewed him to decide whether he should be returned to duty, retained for additional training, recommended for limited service and sent to the replacement depot, or returned to hospital. John hoped for limited service but the board assigned him temporary light duty and reassigned him to the 133d Infantry. He also received a welcome ten-day furlough in Rome, his first extended period of leave since he left the United States.

John returned to the 133d Infantry while his battalion was in the mountains overlooking the Po Valley. Since John had not yet fully recovered, the personnel officer assigned him as a cadre man in the regiment's replacement company.

WAR'S END

While John was away at hospital, his regiment participated in some of the most severe fighting of the Italian campaign, through the Alban Hills and into Rome. They undertook a rapid pursuit of the Germans through Civitavecchia, Tarquinia, San Vincinza, and Cecina, and then into the mountains again to grind against the Gothic Line defenses, finally halting on Mount Belmonte about 10 miles from the Po Valley.

In December John returned to his battalion, at the time based in Loiana. Between December 1944 and March 1945, he rotated with his battalion between rest camps, training and manning the line. Battle casualties were low: only 30 killed, 28 missing, and 109 wounded for the four months; this was fewer than a quarter of the casualties suffered in the three weeks at Cassino or in the days following the breakout at Anzio. In February, John celebrated 22 months in the regiment and three years in service.

By late 1944 the replacements from training centers in the United States were better than those received previously, or even those trained in theater from anti-aircraft and other deactivated units.

Soldiers advance through Tuscany, Italy. Few wear the haversack and most have their sleeping gear rolled into tubes and slung across their shoulders.

Soldiers, supported by an M10 tank destroyer, prepare to cross a berm. The nearest soldier carries the new M1943 entrenching tool attached to his M1945 field pack.

By February 1945, few Guardsmen and initial draftees who had arrived overseas with the 133d Infantry remained in the rifle companies, and they had voluntarily decided to stay. Most of those who remained from its service in Northern Ireland were cooks, clerks, drivers, and some men in the Cannon Company. The last instance of a Guardsman wounded in a line company occurred in October 1944. The rotation policy and casualties had made John one of the oldest men serving in a rifle company, and his time to rotate was approaching.

Some due to rotate were offered promotions if they stayed with the regiment. Lieutenants were promoted to captain, and some enlisted men were battlefield appointed to lieutenant. Officers and enlisted saw these men as more competent than replacement officers from the United States because of their experience. Others were offered NCO rank. John decided to stay when offered the platoon sergeant's position in the weapons platoon.

His commander promoted him to staff sergeant because all the technical sergeant positions were filled by soldiers on furlough, in hospital, and as cadre in the replacement company. In fact, there was only one technical sergeant on the front lines. This was not abnormal, however; every company was like a breathing organism, with men flowing in and out, constantly back and forth between the front and rear.

One of the different things about belonging to a long-service combat outfit was that not many men were court-martialed or listed on morning reports as AWOL. Many veterans believed that since they spent so much time on the line with little complaint, their unit should disregard such minor infractions. What occurred in the rear areas was different from what happened on the line.

A weary member of a heavy machine gun platoon stays awake while men around him sleep. The four machine guns rest against the column, one with a bouquet of flowers in the muzzle.

John knew and understood the silent agreement. His principal duty besides ammunition resupply was sending a daily status report to the first sergeant detailing how many men he had available for duty and the status of those who weren't. He covered for those "old timers" missing in the rear as well as some of the newcomers who had acquitted themselves well on the firing line.

Already familiar with machine guns, John spent some time with the mortar men learning their craft. John learned how to adjust the 60mm mortar fire using the direct alignment method. By staying within 100 yds of the mortars, he could adjust the impact of the rounds using the same mil formula he learned as a machine gunner. Once he sighted a target, he gave the direction in mils and range to the guns. He then adjusted each round's impact using the bracketing method (one round over, one under, and continually splitting the bracket until range was correct) and adjusted the deviation by using the mil reticle in his binoculars until the target was within the bursting radius of the round. Although he enjoyed adjusting the mortars, he was not able to practice as much as he wanted, especially with the shortage of mortar ammunition in the MTO at the time

He found one of the benefits of being responsible for the platoon's resupply was that he had a jeep, and didn't have to walk everywhere, except of course when he did his daily climb up the mountain to his sections' positions. Patrolling was also in the past.

Not every day on the line involved fighting. Soldiers faced with monotony perfected cooking recipes using C and K rations, read and reread letters from home, newspapers, and magazines, and evaluated equipment as only an infantryman could. Life on the line was bad, but not as terrible as the year before had been.

Hot coffee and food, even if only K rations, were lifesavers in the cold. Those on the front lines facing the enemy used heating candles or the much-valued German Esbit stove that burned trioxane fuel.

On the reverse slopes, squads used one-burner Coleman stoves that were about the size of a quart thermos and burned anything from kerosene to gasoline. They were prized possessions and John's friends said they would rather attack without a helmet than leave their stove for the next guy. Soldiers had woolen sweaters, M1943 field jackets, woolen underwear, trigger finger mittens and cushioned woolen socks for the winter of 1944. Those on the front lines also received mountain sleeping bags, shoepacs, cold weather parkas, pile caps, and insulated sleeping pads. As a result of this additional clothing given the soldier on the line, and the increased command emphasis on combating cold weather injuries, trench foot cases reduced by 70 percent.

John and his comrades were happy to wear woolen trousers and shirts. Many thought the herringbone twill uniforms too much the color of the German field uniform. The GI woolen sweater and heavy woolen socks were favorites. John and every other infantryman had two pair of socks, one to wear and one to keep dry inside their shirts, rotating when those worn got wet. The new M1943 field jacket was nice but everyone preferred the zippered combat jacket they wore the year before.

The men on the front lines disliked the sleeping bags because they felt trapped by the zipper and since they couldn't take their boots off, the inside of their bags were soon a muddy mess. After infantrymen throughout Italy complained, the sleeping bags were retrieved and reissued to rear echelon soldiers and the infantrymen received four blankets each. Two men sleeping in a pup tent shared eight blankets. The shoepacs – winter boots with rubber lowers and leather waterproof uppers – were good when the soldiers weren't moving much (like John's mortar men), but they weren't good for sustained walking. The boots lacked arch support, so walking for any distance ruined the feet.

The final offensive in Italy began on April 14, and on the 15th II Corps joined the Fifth Army offensive after a massive bombing and artillery barrage. All of the artillery rounds that had not been fired during the winter months smothered the German defenses and rear areas.

The fighting was not heavy and casualties were light with six killed and 26 wounded for the month in John's company, about 20 percent of the company's authorized strength, but nothing in comparison to some of its past battles. His regiment suffered the loss of only about five percent of its strength. Once Bologna fell on the 21st, it seemed the German defense dissolved, and the GIs could not advance fast enough

German prisoners stream to the rear as the war's end nears.

on foot. Men loaded onto regimental vehicles, vehicles from other units, and captured German vehicles as they sped from Modena to Reggio to Parma. Motorized patrols pushed to the Po River and Mantova, the gateway to the Brenner Pass and Austria. The 133d Infantry then turned westward to liberate Brescia, Bergamo, Milan, and Gallarate. On May 2, John and his company were at Avigniana, just west of Turin, when they heard the war in Italy was over.

On May 9, John and his comrades listened over the radio to President Truman announce the end of the war against Germany:

"The Allied armies, through sacrifice and devotion and with God's help, have wrung from Germany a final and unconditional surrender. The western world has been freed of the evil forces which for five years and longer have imprisoned the bodies and broken the lives of millions upon millions of free-born men. They have violated their churches, destroyed their homes, corrupted their children, and murdered their loved ones. Our Armies of Liberation have restored freedom to these suffering peoples, whose spirit and will the oppressors could never enslave ... For the triumph of spirit and of arms which we have won, and for its promise to peoples everywhere who join us in the love of freedom, it is fitting that we, as a nation, give thanks to Almighty God, who has strengthened us and given us victory."

The war in Europe was over. After fighting for almost three years in the Mediterranean, John thought of home.

GOING HOME

In mid-May, John and his comrades read in the *Stars and Stripes* that men with more than 85 points were going home. Knowing he was leaving soon, John listened to some of his men just below the cut bemoan the fact that they weren't awarded a Purple Heart when they had been wounded without going to hospital. Purple Hearts and decorations weren't important while in combat but they meant a great deal with the war over and men wanting to go home. Many orders were cut that retroactively granted soldiers Purple Hearts for earlier wounds and other awards that had gone without action during combat.

Most of the soldiers who traveled overseas in January 1942 were long gone, as were most who had arrived in Tunisia. Every soldier who had traveled overseas in January 1942 had more than 80 points of service and overseas credit alone. Moreover, when campaigns, medals, wounds, and children were added, some had as many as 120 points. The high

Adjusted Service Rating, based on a number of factors including time in service, time overseas, combat service, and parenthood (War Department Press Release May 10, 1945).

Group	Remarks	John's points
1. Service credit	1 point per month in the service since September 16, 1940	40 x 1 = 40
2. Overseas credit	1 point per month overseas since September 16, 1940	31 x 1 = 31
3. a) Combat credits	5 points for every Bronze Service Star (battle participation stars)	5 x 6 = 30
3. b) Decorations	5 points for the first and each additional award of the following for service performed since September 16, 1940. (Distinguished Service Cross, Distinguished Service Medal, Legion of Merit, Silver Star, Distinguished Flying Cross, Soldier's Medal, Bronze Star, Air Medal)	1 x 5 = 5
3. c) Number of wounds	5 points per wound as recognized by award of Purple Heart	1 x 5 = 5
4. Parenthood credit	12 points per child under 18 years up to a limit of three children	0
TOTAL		**111**

casualties in 1943 and 1944 and the rotation policy meant that most of the men in his company were recent arrivals, with the great majority arriving in the months after Cassino. Most had four campaigns, 13 months of overseas credit, and 18 months of service, giving them 51 points plus the points for wounds, decorations, and parenthood.

John left in May with other high pointers from all the divisions. On the left breast of his Eisenhower jacket he proudly wore his Combat Infantryman's Badge, Bronze Star, Purple Heart, and the European, African, Middle Eastern Campaign Medal with six Bronze Service Stars, one for each campaign he participated in. On his left sleeve were the 34th Infantry Division patch, staff sergeant stripes, five overseas service bars, each denoting six months, and one service stripe for three years of service.

New replacements and men from divisions returning to the United States in the summer, themselves high-point men from other units, replaced those leaving. The War Department reduced the points required to go home to 80 points early in September, 70 on October 1, and 60 points on November 1.

The 133d Infantry Regiment deployed overseas in January 1942, entered combat in late March 1943, and suffered casualties higher than most other regiments deployed to the Mediterranean. The average infantry regiment in the MTO lost 41 officers and 668 enlisted men killed, 133 officers and 2,413 enlisted wounded. In approximately 27 months of combat, the 133d Infantry Regiment lost 47 officers and 998 enlisted men killed, 18 officers and 449 enlisted men missing or captured, and 188 officers and 4,060 enlisted men wounded, most of whom were lost at Cassino and after the Anzio breakout. This did not include the thousands of nonbattle casualties due to trench foot, frostbite, combat fatigue or other illnesses.

The price of success in the Mediterranean amounted to 106,131 battle casualties in the 12 Army infantry divisions deployed to the MTO at some period during the war. In 446 months of infantry regiment combat, 19,719 men (18.5 percent of total battle casualties) were killed.

The 133d Infantry Regiment departed Italy aboard the USS *Monticello* on October 22, and arrived in Hampton Roads, Virginia in November. Only a few of the men present when the regiment shipped overseas in January 1942 came home with the regiment's colors, and of those, most were in headquarters or support companies. The men in the rifle and weapons companies had been earlier evacuated for wounds or injuries, shipped home as high pointers on furlough or discharge in May and June 1945, or buried in cemeteries in Tunisia and throughout Italy.

John's awards: (a) Combat Infantryman Badge; (b) Bronze Star; (c) Purple Heart; and (d) European, African, Middle Eastern Campaign medal with six battle stars.

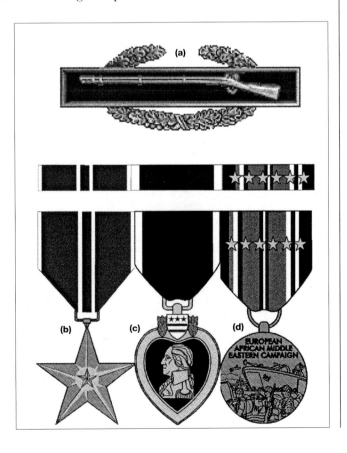

ABOVE **A Mediterranean war cemetery.**

John sat at home on furlough awaiting his discharge. He was sure that his would be on white parchment, signifying an Honorable Discharge under excellent, very good, or good conduct. He was sure his few days of AWOL back in 1942 would not be enough to change the color of his discharge to blue, which represented a General Discharge for ineptness or misconduct. He knew of only one man to have received a yellow, or Dishonorable Discharge, which was after his general courtmartial.

Once John was home, he sat in the quiet, not knowing what to do. He missed the camaraderie and adrenalin rush of active service. He surely would not be able to live as he had before the war; he had seen and done too much. So, rather than go back to farming, he re-enlisted: "I was with the 34th Division in Tunisia and Italy. First battalion of the One-Three-Three."

RIGHT **133d Infantry Regiment battle casualties, Mediterranean Theater of Operations.**

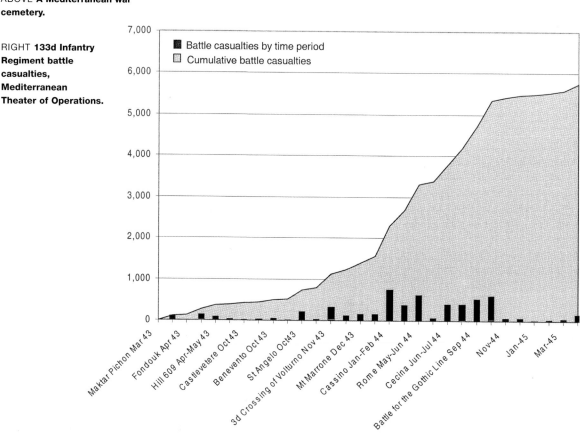

Division	Component federalized	Organized / Overseas	Arrived Combat	First in MTO	Campaigns	Deaths	Wounded	Captured
*1	RA	May 1917	Aug 7, 1942	Nov 1942	3	2392	3760	1266
*3	RA	Nov 1917	Nov 8, 1942	Nov 1942	6	3162	9277	1665
*9	RA	Aug 1940	Nov 8, 1942	Nov 1942	3	1645	3350	780
34	NG	Feb 1941	Jan 31, 1942	Nov 1942	6	3408	11545	1368
*45	NG	Feb 1940	Jun 22, 1943	Jul 1943	4	2650	7195	2261
*82 Abn	RA	Mar 1942	May 10, 1943	Jul 1943	2	1992	6560	615
*36	NG	Nov 1940	Apr 13, 1943	Sep 1943	7	3717	13191	2650
88	AUS	Jul 1942	Dec 15, 1943	Feb 1944	3	2606	9225	647
85	AUS	May 1942	Jan 2, 1944	Mar 1944	3	1775	6314	497
91	AUS	Aug 1942	Apr 21, 1944	Jun 1944	3	1581	6748	334
92	AUS	Oct 1942	Oct 16, 1944	Aug 1944	2	624	2187	56
10 Mtn	RA	Jul 1943	Jan 8, 4195	Jan 1945	2	955	3134	28

* Later served in European Theater of Operations.

MUSEUMS, RE-ENACTMENT AND COLLECTING

ABOVE **US infantry division losses in the Mediterranean Theater of Operations.**

The museums below have information on the 133d Infantry Regiment and the infantryman's war in the MTO.

Iowa Gold Star Museum, 7700 Northwest Beaver Drive, Johnston, Iowa 50131. Tel: (515) 252 4531

The National Infantry Museum, Bldg 396, Fort Benning, Georgia. Tel: (706) 545 6762

Reference websites:

http://www.reenactor.net/ww2/ww2ring.html (WWII Reenactors Web Ring)

http://www.army.mil/cmh-pg/museums/musdir.htm (US Army Center of Military History)

BIBLIOGRAPHY

Primary

Appel, J W MD, *Prevention of Manpower Loss from Psychiatric Disorders*, March 22, 1945 (unpublished study)

US Army Military History Institute, *WWII History, 133d Infantry, 34th Infantry Division*, file #603–133, 1945

Headquarters, 133d Infantry Regiment, S3 Operation Report. n.p. NARA RG 407. 334–INF(133)–0.3
133d Regiment History n.p. NARA RG 407.334–INF(133)–0.3

Roster of killed and died: 133d Infantry Regiment, NARA

US Department of Army, Adjutant General's Office. *Army Battle Casualties and Nonbattle Deaths in World War II: Final Report, December 7, 1941 to December 31, 1946*, Government Printing Office, Washington, DC (June 1953)

FM 7–5 *Organization and Tactics of Infantry; the Rifle Battalion, 1940*, Government Printing Office, Washington, DC, 1940

FM 7–10 *Rifle Company, Rifle Regiment, June 2, 1942*, Government Printing Office, Washington, DC, 1942

FM 7–15 *Heavy Weapons Company, Rifle Regiment, May 19, 1942*, Government Printing Office, Washington, DC, 1942

FM 7–40 *Rifle Regiment, February 9, 1942*, Government Printing Office, Washington, DC, 1942

FM 21–5 *Military Training, July 16, 1941*, Government Printing Office, Washington, DC, 1941

FM 21–100 *Soldier's Handbook, December 11, 1940*, Government Printing Office, Washington, DC, 1941

FM 22–5 *Infantry Drill Regulations*, Government Printing Office, Washington, DC, 1939 and 1941

FM 100–5 *Operations, May 22, 1941*, Government Printing Office, Washington, DC, 1941

Secondary

Ankrum, H R *Dogfaces Who Smiled Through Tears: The 34th Red Bull Infantry Division*, Graphic Publishing Company, Lake Mills, Iowa, 1987

Blumenson, M *Salerno to Cassino* Government Printing Office, Washington, DC, 1969–1988

Fisher, E F *Cassino to the Alps* Government Printing Office, Washington, DC (1977–1989)

Howe, G F *Northwest Africa: seizing the initiative in the West* Government Printing Office, Washington, DC, 1957–1991

Linderman, G F *The World Within War: America's Combat Experience in World War II*. The Free Press New York, 1997

McCarthy, J 'Iron-Man Battalion,' *Yank Magazine, European Edition, Vol 1:38*, pp 2–5, December 22, 1944, Great Britain

Palmer, R R, Wiley, B I, and Keast, W R *The Procurement and Training of Ground Combat Troops The Army Ground Forces, US Army in World War II*. Government Printing Office, Washington, DC, 1948

Pyle, E *Brave Men*, Henry Holt and Company, Inc. New York, 1944

War Department, *Anzio Beachhead January 22–May 25, 1944* Government Printing Office, Washington, DC, 1948, 1990

War Department, *5th Army at the Winter Line (November 15, 1943– January 15, 1944)*, Government Printing Office, Washington, DC, 1945, 1990

War Department, *From the Volturno to the Winter Line October 6–November 15, 1943*, Government Printing Office, Washington, DC, 1945, 1990

War Department, *Salerno, American operations from the beaches to the Volturno (September 9–October 6, 1943)*, Government Printing Office, Washington, DC, 1944, 1990

War Department, *To Bizerte with the II Corps, April 23, 1943–May 13, 1943*. Government Printing Office, Washington, DC, 1944, 1990

Wiltse, C M *The Medical Department: Medical Service in the Mediterranean and Minor Theaters*, Government Printing Office, Washington, DC, 1987, 1965

A World War II and 'Cold War' Mediterranean Retrospective
http://www.milhist.net/index.html#mto

History of the 34th ("Red Bull") Infantry Division
http://www.dma.state.mn.us/redbull/HISTORY/History.htm

COLOR PLATE COMMENTARY

PLATE A: TRAINING AT CAMP WHEELER, GEORGIA, MARCH 1942

This illustration shows a standard speed-type obstacle course, which "John" completed in March 1942 during training at Camp Wheeler, Georgia. The course measured a soldier's endurance and agility, and the 100-yd course (shown in shortened perspecitve at the top of the illustration) was run during the third week. The soldiers shown carry M1903 Springfield rifles with affixed M1905 bayonet and bear M1928 haversacks. The men had to hurdle two fences, run through a maze (1), scale a 7ft high wall (2), crawl under a trestle (3), leap across a ditch, run across elevated wood beams (4), and then sprint to the finish line. The course developed stamina, fitness, and coordination, and the soldiers would compete against each other to see who could record the fastest time.

PLATE B: JOHN AS A RIFLEMAN, 1ST BATTALION 133D INFANTRY REGIMENT, TUNISIA, MARCH 1943

John is shown here in front and rear views aged 20: he has recently arrived in North Africa and is about to enter first combat. He wears the Parson's jacket, with the "Red Bull" 34th Infantry Division patch (1) on his left shoulder (the 133d Infantry Regiment crest is also shown, 2), and the First Pattern Herringbone Twill (HBT) trousers: to keep warm, he wears his woolen brown trousers under these, as well as a thick woolen brown shirt under his jacket. He wears standard issue boots and canvas leggings, and the M1 helmet.

John carries the M2A2 gas mask (3) and bag (4), and is armed with the M1 Garand rifle (5): a detail of one 8-round clip (6), one .30 cal. bullet (7), and how to load the clip into the rifle (8) are also shown. John's M1 helmet (9) is shown in full detail, comprising the inner composite liner (10) and strap (11), the outer steel shell (12) and chinstrap (13, with an exploded view of the buckle, 14), and the lining headband (15). John also bears the M1928 haversack (16), with the M1910 entrenching tool (17) and a bayonet attached.

John is also equipped with the five-pocket M1928 cartridge belt (18), with a canteen (19) and the M1910 first-aid pouch (20) attached. Also shown are the M1936 suspenders (21): these were attached to the belt to give support for heavier items carried.

PLATE C: RIFLE COMPANY ORGANIZATION, 1943

Rifle company organisation chart: as in 1942 the rifle

company contained three platoons of three squads each with 12 infantrymen plus a five-man headquarters element; a weapons platoon with a mortar section consisting of three 60mm mortars and a machine gun section containing two M1919A3 .30 cal. light machine guns. (See Warrior 45 *US Infantryman in World War II (1) Pacific Area of Operations 1941–45* for an organizational diagram of the Rifle Company TO&E for 1941; and Warrior 56: *US Infantryman in World War II (3) European Theater of Operations 1944–45* for an organizational diagram of the Rifle Company TO&E for 1944.)

Platoon formations: the four basic movement formations for infantry platoons were: Platoon column, which was easy to control and best for movement in woods, through smoke, at night, and through defiles and along trails; Platoon on line, which allowed greatest firepower forward and was usually used during the assault phase of an attack; Platoon "V" with the bulk of the firepower to the front and flanks and balanced movement and control; and the Platoon wedge, which was used when the enemy situation was uncertain and provided a high degree of flexibility and control.

PLATE D: HEAVY WEAPONS COMPANY, 1943–44

The company comprised two heavy machine gun platoons of two sections of two machine guns each, and an 81mm mortar platoon of three sections of two mortars each. The M1 81mm mortar and M1917A1 water-cooled Browning machine gun remained the weapons systems in the rifle battalion heavy weapons companies throughout the war. The Browning .50 cal. machine gun also served the company at headquarters level.

PLATE E: HEAVY WEAPONS POSITIONS

Top illustration: this shows the dug-in position for an M1917A1 water-cooled heavy machine gun, from several different views. The gunner fires the weapon, and the assistant gunner next to him feeds the ammunition (note that the assistant gunner has been removed from the illustration so as to show the gunner's position more clearly.)

The bottom illustration: this shows the dug-in position for an 81mm mortar, from several different views. The World War II mortars did not have 360 degree traverse as do current mortars, allowing the positions to be much smaller. A vignette shows the angle of maximum traverse of the mortar. The assistant gunner loads the shell into the mortar, and the gunner aims it and adjusts firing.

PLATE F: MONTE CASSINO HOUSE CLEARING, 1944

This illustration is set in the battle for Monte Cassino, Italy, in January 1944, and shows four stages of how to clear a house of German troops.

1. An M4A2 Sherman tank blasts the house at close range to create an entry point and suppress enemy defensive fire. The lead attacking men stay under cover.

2. The first group of three American infantrymen move quickly from cover, and toss grenades through the ground floor door and windows. The other infantrymen have their rifles trained on the house to cover them.

3. Other infantrymen launch rifle grenades into the top floor windows, aiming to drive the enemy there down to ground level: they also watch for German soldiers appearing at the upper windows.

4. The remaining enemy occupiers surrender to the men on ground floor: the second group of American infantry and the tank move on to the next house, leaving the first group to secure the house and prevent enemy reoccupation.

PLATE G: 60MM MORTAR SQUAD

This plate shows a 60mm mortar squad from the 34th Infantry in action. There are five soldiers in each mortar squad, as follows. The Squad Leader (1, a corporal) selects the firing position, and observes and adjusts fire. He has a pair of binoculars around his kneck, and is shown communicating on a walkie-talkie. The gunner (2) carries the mortar, aims and sets its elevation, and ensures the sight levels are correct. The assistant gunner (3) feeds the ammunition. Both the gunner and assistant gunner are armed with the M1911 .45 cal. pistol. The two ammunition bearers (4 and 5) carry the mortar ammunition, normally six rounds each in containers. They are armed with M1 carbine rifles.

The 60mm mortar is 28.6 in (72.6 cm) long, and weighs 42 lbs (19.05 kg) fully assembled. Two small diagrams show the maximum and minimum angles of elevation (6) and traverse (7) of the mortar. It is aimed using the M4 sight (8). This small instrument, weighing 1.16 lb (0.52 kg) uses a collimator instead of a telescope. The sight is mounted on the M2 mortar bipod (9), shown here without the mortar attached. Also shown is one shell (10): the range of each is approximately between 100 yds and 1,985 yds (91.44 m and 1,815 m).

PLATE H: JOHN, STAFF SERGEANT, ITALY, EARLY 1945

John is now 22 years old, and his equipment and demeanor have changed dramatically since 1942. A combat hardened and weary veteran, he is bearded and has a grimy face from huddling around oil stoves on an Italian mountainside.

He wears the M1943 field jacket (1) with M1943 pile liner (2). His jacket displays the 34th Infantry Division patch on the left shoulder, Staff Sergeant stripes on his left sleeve, and the blue Combat Infantryman's Badge above his left breast pocket. He wears the woolen Enlisted Men's trousers, tucked into his M1944 Shoepac boots (3). He also wears brown woolen gloves and the M1 helmet, which has a small "Red Bull" painted on its front. Under his helmet he wears the wool knit cap (4). John is armed with the M1 .30 cal. carbine, and wears the M1936 belt, with M1 carbine ammunition pouches attached. Also hooked on are a canteen and first aid kit pouch.

On his back he carries the M1944 combat field pack with cargo pack attached below (5). Attached to this are the M1943 entrenching tool (6, the cover is also shown) and blanket roll.

Also shown is a dinner ration kit (7), together with its contents. These are (a) a K-2 biscuit, (b) a tin of processed cheese, (c) a K-1 biscuit, (d) a fruit bar, (e) chewing gum, (f) lemon juice powder, (g) a pack of four cigarettes, and (h) sugar tablets.

INDEX

Figures in **bold** refer to illustrations